Praise for *The Writer's Book of Hope*

"Ralph Keyes has done it again: he's written an indispensable book for the nervous writer and all writers are nervous. Informative, sometimes hilarious, and always wise and sympathetic, it will be an enormous help to any writer and a lifesaver to the beginner. A wonderful book."

—Patrick O'Connor, editor, author of *Don't Look Back*

"Ralph Keyes is the best kind of coach: practical, encouraging, and honest. *The Writer's Book of Hope* is a perfect blend of inspiration and no-nonsense guidance, sure to speed the journey from empty page to publication."

—Philip Goldberg, author of *Roadsigns:*
Navigating Your Path to Spiritual Happiness

"After publishing four novels, I'm wondering why I still get Dark Terrors every time I sit down to write, why the publishing process seems shrouded in mysticism, and why I crave encouragement like a tail-wagging puppy. So along comes *The Writer's Book of Hope* to tell me that angst and rejection are normal, even desirable; that I shouldn't worry that the publishing business doesn't make much sense; and that despair and hope can co-exist quite nicely. If you're a writer or ever even thought about writing, read this book."

—Robert Inman, author of *Captain Saturday*

"Every writer needs a friend. Ralph Keyes's new book is that and more. *The Writer's Book of Hope* is destined to become an instant classic."

—Eva Shaw, Ph.D., writing teacher and author of *Writeriffic:*
Creativity Training for Writers

"Pulling together hundreds of writers' stories and reflections, Ralph Keyes weaves a blanket of hope that you can wrap around your shoulders whenever the cold winds of self-doubt come calling. I myself plan to keep this book nearby and take regular doses of 'hope' vitamins."

—Rosalie Maggio, author of *How to Say It*

"Every writer who is dreaming of publication or who is currently dealing with publishers needs to read *The Writer's Book of Hope*. Keyes's insights into the world of 'pub people' is refreshingly honest and humorous. A veteran writer himself, Keyes encourages other writers by making us feel valued and by putting our frustrations into perspective. This book is an excellent companion to *The Courage to Write*, and one I recommend to all writers and students of writing."

—Anthony Grooms, professor of creative writing,
Kennesaw State University and author of *Bombingham*

"After reading *The Writer's Book of Hope* I felt as though I'd just attended an inspiring, supportive writers' conference. Ralph Keyes offers specific advice I've seen addressed in no other book—not so much on how to write as how to keep writing. *The Writer's Book of Hope* devotes an entire chapter to the 'encouragers' a writer needs in her life. This book now goes to the top of my own list of encouragers."

—Katrina Kittle, author of *Two Truths and a Lie*

"No one knows the lonely, exhilarating, and terrifying world of writers better than Ralph Keyes! As with his earlier book, *The Courage to Write*, Keyes provides us with string for the labyrinth of a writer's day and professional life. I'll recommend *The Writer's Book of Hope* to writers and non-writers alike—its wisdom, hopefulness, and practicality will inspire all."

—Julie Alvarez, author of
How the García Girls Lost Their Accents

Also by Ralph Keyes

Chancing It: Why We Take Risks

The Courage to Write: How Writers Transcend Fear

The Height of Your Life

The Innovation Paradox:
The Success of Failure, the Failure of Success
(coauthored with Richard Farson)

Is There Life after High School?

"Nice Guys Finish Seventh": False Phrases,
Spurious Sayings, and Familiar Misquotations

Sons on Fathers: A Book of Men's Writing

Timelock: How Life Got So Hectic
and What You Can Do about It

We, the Lonely People: Searching for Community

The Wit and Wisdom of Harry Truman

The Wit and Wisdom of Oscar Wilde

The Writer's Book of Hope

THE
WRITER'S
BOOK OF
HOPE

GETTING FROM
FRUSTRATION
TO PUBLICATION

RALPH KEYES

An Owl Book

HENRY HOLT AND COMPANY · NEW YORK

For my friends
Lou and Jonellen Heckler,
who have always encouraged me

Owl Books
Henry Holt and Company, LLC
Publishers since 1866
175 Fifth Avenue
New York, New York 10010
www.henryholt.com

An Owl Book® and ®are registered trademarks
of Henry Holt and Company, LLC.

Library of Congress Cataloging-in-Publication Data

Keyes, Ralph.
  The writer's book of hope : getting from frustration
to publication / Ralph Keyes.—1st ed.
    p.   cm.
  ISBN-13: 978-0-8050-7235-8
  ISBN-10: 0-8050-7235-7
    1. Authorship—Psychological aspects.   2. Authorship—Marketing.
I. Title.

PN171.P83K54   2003
808'.02'019—dc21   2003042332

Henry Holt books are available for special promotions
and premiums. For details contact: Director, Special Markets.

First Edition 2003

Designed by Victoria Hartman

Printed in the United States of America
5 7 9 10 8 6 4

Contents

II · LOOKING OUT

III · BEYOND FRUSTRATION

Acknowledgments

Judith Appelbaum encouraged me to write this book as she's encouraged me to write many others, and I can't thank her enough. She is the quintessential *encourager* (see chapter 8).

Judy also gave me helpful feedback on the completed manuscript, as did Andi Adkins, Susan DeBow, Joe Downing, Pat Gaudette, Jonellen Heckler, Muriel Keyes, Rosalie Maggio, Meena Nayak, Phil Offen, Kathryn Olney, and Mary Tom Watts. Andi, Jonellen, and Judy also reviewed the original proposal for the book, as did Gay Courter, William Phillips, and Patrick O'Connor. My agent, Michelle Tessler, gave me a good hand with the book's proposal, then capably arranged its publication. This book is better for the judicious editing of Senior Editor Deborah Brody at Henry Holt, and careful copyediting of Victoria Haire.

Helpful suggestions along the way were made by my brother Gene Keyes, and friends Gay Courter and Lou Heckler.

Librarians at the Yellow Springs and Antioch College libraries were their usual helpful selves, especially Connie Collett.

As ever, my wife, Muriel, has been my best source of ongoing support.

By creating and maintaining such a great Web site for me, my sons, David and Scott, made it easier for their father to stay in touch with colleagues and readers.

I would especially like to thank the many readers of *The Courage to Write* who took the time to respond, and by doing so encouraged me to write this sequel.

Sit at desk. Examine blank computer screen. Cursor blinks impatiently. Small fan hums within. Neighbor fires up leaf blower. Mail truck rumbles by. Kid's voice pierces closed door: "Matthew hit me!" Spouse opens door, mail in hand. Hands over two manila envelopes addressed to you in your own handwriting. Spouse wonders when you'll be ready to quit. When indeed?

{ I }

LOOKING
IN

·1·

The Essential Ingredient

Call him John. Even though John's job paid well enough, he found it boring and unsatisfying. John dreamed of becoming a writer. Eventually, he decided to stop dreaming and start writing. This meant getting up at five every morning so he could go to work early and scribble fiction on a yellow legal pad. At night John would squeeze out another page or two on an old Smith-Corona word processor resting on a board wedged between the washer and dryer in the laundry room of a three-bedroom ranch home he shared with his wife and infant son. This made for slow going. John thought often about giving up on writing as an impossible dream. He didn't, however, and after three years of early morning and late night writing had a book-length manuscript.

John sent his manuscript to dozens of literary agents and publishers whose names he got from a guidebook. All sent it back. An agent finally agreed to take him on, one not considered particularly prestigious in the status-conscious world of publishing. After several more rejections, this agent sold John's novel to an obscure publisher in Connecticut. That publisher paid a modest advance, then sold very few of the 5,000 copies of John's book that it had printed. In the meantime he'd completed a second novel. His agent had trouble selling that one too. John saw little room for hope and wondered whether it was finally time to throw in the towel. Until—but I get ahead of my story. Let's come back to it later.

Does John's story sound familiar? Like your own in certain respects? If so, you are not alone. Frustration is the natural habitat of writers at every level. I've felt it. So did John. So does anyone who aspires to write.

I've noticed this especially while speaking at writers' courses and conferences. Antsiness fills the air like ions before a thunderstorm. Participants worry about lacking talent. Their submissions get rejected. Inspiration wanes. It all seems so futile. Why keep going?

Without being Pollyannish, I try to reassure these fledgling writers. Hang in there, I say. You'd be surprised by how many successful writers were once discouraged ones. Did you know that Samuel Beckett's first novel was rejected by forty-two publishers? That a dozen agents chose not to represent J. K. Rowling? That Beatrix Potter had to self-publish *The Tale of Peter Rabbit*? These are good grounds for hope. There are many more.

Is Hope Necessary?

Any writer has a legitimate, valid need to hear that it isn't all for naught. This may sound self-evident, but it isn't to everyone. Some of my colleagues even try to discourage new writers, on the theory that anyone who can be driven out of the business this way shouldn't be there in the first place. They seem to feel that admitting a need for encouragement suggests one is too wimpy to be a writer. Writing isn't for sissies, they say. If you can't stand the grief, get out of the profession. Even Anne Lamott—whose delightful book *Bird by Bird* touched on writing despair—once despaired herself that addressing a writ-ers' conference meant offering "hope-to-the-hopeless."

Gee. That's awfully harsh. I've been involved with such a conference—the Antioch Writers' Workshop—for nearly two decades. Every year at least one of our graduates has sold a book to the likes of Knopf, HarperCollins, Warner, and Gray-wolf. Others have had scripts produced, stories anthologized, and articles published. The help we give these authors-in-the-making lies less in the realm of metaphors or marketing tactics than the simple *idea* that it's possible to write and get pub-lished. You *can* be a writer, we tell them. That message alone is worth the price of admission.

Unfortunately, the most daunting problems writers face are seldom considered at courses and conferences. These gatherings usually emphasize basic principles of good writing: show, don't tell; use active verbs; be sparing with adjectives and adverbs; make effective use of detail. Students learn about story struc-ture and pacing and transitions and point of view. Advice is given on how to approach publishers. Such lessons are valuable, even invaluable. But mastering the elements of style can't pro-duce the will to keep writing. The hardest part of being a writer is not getting your commas in the right place but getting your head in the right place. Where help is really needed is in the area of countering anxiety, frustration, and despair.

In his encouraging book *On Writing: A Memoir of the Craft*, Stephen King admitted, "Confidence during the actual writing of this book was a commodity in remarkably short supply. What I was long on was physical pain and self-doubt." Like King, all writers need encouragement, at every step of their career—even those who win the Nobel Prize for literature. If anyone should be beyond the need for validation it's a Nobel laureate like Saul Bel-low. Yet, according to Bellow's longtime agent Harriet Wasser-man, during the years that she represented him, reassurance was exactly what he craved—constantly. After each novel, no matter how well received, Bellow was like a fledgling writer, hungry for the least scrap of reassurance. Even after he won the Nobel, every book Bellow wrote was like a maiden effort. As Wasserman put it, "For Saul, every book is his first book, and he is always the first-time writer welcoming reenforcement."

There is not a writer alive who couldn't use a dose of reassurance. This has nothing to do with the quality of their work or the stage of their career. Regardless of how much one may have published, writing—books especially—is such an enervating experience that it is hard to keep the words coming without getting an occasional "You go, girl!" A word or two of encouragement can keep writers at their desks when all seems for naught. At those times, reassurance is far more helpful than marketing tips or style pointers.

This is a point of near-consensus among humane teacher-writers. The evidence can be found in their own careers. While making $6,000 a year as a young freshman composition teacher at Colgate University, Frederick Busch received constant encouragement for a novel in progress from an editor at Atlantic Monthly Press. Even though she didn't accept his novel, late in a successful career Busch still remembered the reassurance he got from this woman when he felt so unsure of himself. In Busch's words, "That sort of encouragement is underrated, usually by the writers who have received it, but it is stupendously important. . . . You know it's not all over, you know it is one day going to be wonderful, and you know that someone's caring for you—you are *not*, in a cruel profession, alone."

Isn't that the real reason we attend those writing conferences and take courses on writing and read books on the subject? To feel less alone with our self-doubt? We're not looking for tips on how to write so much as reasons to keep writing. And we should. How can you write without hope? Hope is the essential ingredient, as crucial to a writer as similes and semicolons. A simple nod of reassurance can keep us going when every nerve ending says, STOP! ENOUGH! I SURRENDER! We can write without a computer, typewriter, desk, pen, or even paper (some excellent writing has been done in prisons on matchbook covers and toilet tissue). The one thing we can't write without is hope. Hope is to writers as oxygen is to scuba divers. No writer can survive without it.

I once talked with veteran writer William Zinsser just after he'd received several pages of suggested manuscript revisions from his longtime editor at HarperCollins. Despite being the author of fourteen books and scores of articles and essays, despite having been executive editor of the Book-of-the-Month Club and a longtime teacher of writing—as well as the author of two books on the subject, including the much-assigned *On Writing Well*—Zinsser was taken aback. He searched in vain for any words of reassurance in his editor's commentary. Did this man *like* the manuscript? That was the first question Zinsser put to his editor, followed by remonstration for not including any encouraging words in his critique. "Don't think just because I've been doing this so long I don't need encouragement," said Zinsser.

The Ethics of Encouragement

Something I've discussed often with colleagues is whether it's honorable to encourage fledgling writers when we know the odds against them are so great, and the path to publication is so torturous. The problem is that we have no idea which ones will complete this marathon. Anyone who works with writers is continually surprised by who reaches the finish line and who doesn't. Our powers of prediction are not that accurate.

When they were senior editors at Doubleday, Loretta Barrett and Betty Prashker tried to get Barrett's assistant to give up her dream of writing fiction. Based on their reading of a novel the young woman had spent a year and a half writing, both felt confident that she had no future as a novelist. The woman ignored them and went on to publish several books, eventually for six-figure advances that Barrett herself—now an agent— negotiated for her former assistant. Her name? Laura Van Wormer, author of the bestselling series featuring reporter Sally Harrington.

"While it may seem disingenuous to encourage a writer who seems to have no native ability," wrote editor-turned-agent Betsy Lerner in her excellent book *The Forest for the Trees: An Editor's Advice to Writers*, "it is also arrogant to think we know how any given career will develop, or what combination of desire and will may result in a work that will have a profound effect on people even if it is never praised for its beautiful prose."

Lerner knew a writing teacher who went out of her way to be supportive of students' work regardless of its apparent prospects. Why? Because over time she'd so often seen students who seemed hopeless at the outset of a writing class produce outstanding work by the end. This is a common discovery among those who teach writing. During his years of working with aspiring writers at the University of Virginia, novelist George Garrett repeatedly saw his best students become unproductive graduates, while ones for whom he held little hope blossomed into publishing authors. That's why, Garrett concluded, "it's not our duty to discourage."

This certainly has been my experience. After decades of working with aspiring writers, I've realized that it's futile (to say nothing of presumptuous) to try to anticipate who should be encouraged and who shouldn't. Since I have no idea which writers will stay the course and which ones won't, I encourage them all. (This is not the same thing as praising mediocre work.) And for good reason.

After a book and author banquet in Charlotte, North Carolina, a television talk show host named Lou Heckler, who had interviewed me earlier that day, introduced me to his wife, Jonellen. She had some writing in the works, Lou told me. Mrs. Heckler looked shyly at the floor as her husband said this. Her manner was demure, soft-spoken, and reserved. Not dynamic. I gave Mrs. Heckler my standard spiel about hoping she'd stay with it, and that eventually I'd see her byline. To my astonishment, I did: in *Ladies' Home Journal* and other magazines where Jonellen Heckler's short stories and poems began to appear regularly. The next thing I knew, a novel by Jonellen Heckler was in bookstores, followed by a second, a third, and more to come. One of those novels was made into a movie for television. All from a shy aspiring writer whom I'd encouraged because I try—within the boundaries of honesty and credibility—never to be discouraging.

Honest Reassurance

A phrase I like in John Gardner's *On Becoming a Novelist* is "honest reassurance." That's what I hope this book will offer. It is rooted in my own three-plus decades as a writer. This experience has included plenty of frustration and despair. In the process I've discovered realistic grounds for hope, which I'd like to share with you. They are rooted in stories of writers who felt lost at sea but kept rowing long enough to land safely on shore. The point of such stories is to show that it is possible not only to endure but to prevail, as so many writers already have, including some who became well-known authors.

It may not be possible to overcome frustration, but you can learn to live with writing's many aggravations, even make use of them. The implicit message of too many books on writing is: "If only you'd (read more/market better/do affirmations, etc.), you'd become a better writer and conquer your frustration. This one has a different premise. Writing is inherently frustrating. Frustration is part of the literary territory. I won't try to pep-talk you out of feeling discouraged. (Nor would I want to. As we'll see, feeling discouraged can be a positive sign.) Rather, I will suggest informed, realistic reasons to carry on when all seems for naught. I won't pull your leg about success being just over the horizon. I don't have ten surefire ways to get published, or even five. I can tell you what's involved, suggest ways to cope with feelings of frustration, and offer tangible reasons not to put down your pen or turn off your computer— realistic grounds for hope.

This book will not imply that writing is an easy pursuit with a happy outcome likely. It isn't. Nor will it suggest that its author has a formula for publishing success. I don't. Some aspiring writers give the impression that they're looking for a "key," some wisdom known only to insiders on how to write and get published. There is none. The only key is persistence and knowing what you're about. If it's a smooth sail you're looking for, *stop writing immediately*. When it comes to writing, there's no smooth sailing. The literary seas are all rough. Many writers get needlessly discouraged, however, and for the wrong reasons. Some turn back when they should keep sailing. This book is about reasons to persevere. There *is* hope.

The Meaning of Hope

What do I mean by *hope*? As I'll use that term, *hope* is not synonymous with *blind faith*. Even though it is rooted in the spirit, hope can have practical legs to stand on. Faith is part of hope, of course, but it needn't be blind. We're better off when it isn't. That's why this book is about both spiritual *and* practical grounds for not giving up. I've tried to make *The Writer's Book of*

Hope as encouraging as possible, within reason, basing it on tangible grounds for optimism that aren't always evident to writers when they're mired in black lagoons of despair. My goal is to cast light on some of the darker aspects of writing, publication especially, and in the process make them less intimidating.

A lot of books are available, some of them quite good, on practical ways to become a better writer. Another genre is meant to elevate the spirit, without being practical-minded. This one integrates the two, blending consideration of a writer's inner world with the outer one. It is grounded in the experience of working writers, based on voices of experience, including that of the author—a longtime writer who's known his own despair. I'll speak from my perspective as a writer who has published frequently but whose work has been rejected even more frequently.

Early in my career I decided to keep a log in which I recorded my submissions: where they had been sent, when, and what happened to them—a green check mark for acceptance, a red one for rejection. This log recorded lots of red check marks, and very few green ones. Any behavioral psychologist could have told me that this was a surefire way to demoralize myself. Psychologically speaking, my log-keeping method violated a basic tenet of behavioral conditioning: recognize results you want to reinforce, ignore everything else. That's why I stopped keeping a log.

An aspiring author* once asked me what trait would help most in her dream of becoming a writer. Without thinking, I responded, "A high tolerance for humiliation." This was not flippant. Like most writers, I've had to endure excruciating lows alternating with exhilarating highs. My publisher had high hopes

---

*With exceptions noted in the notes, anonymous sources asked not to be identified, or spoke to me in private conversations. When first names only are used to identify those I write about, they are pseudonyms.

for my third book and did a substantial first printing. Sales did not meet expectations, however, and much of that printing was eventually closed out as "remainders." Bookstores were not the only ones to buy them. Several dozen also showed up at the IKEA furniture superstore in Philadelphia where customers looking for chairs and sofas could reflect on why so many copies of an author's book had become ornamental objects in a furniture store's bookcases instead of being for sale in a bookstore.

This was one of many downcast moments when I felt I had little reason to keep going other than the hope that things would get better. And they did. After that low point I published eight more books, including *The Courage to Write*. That book focused on fear. This one moves along to frustration. Once we've faced our fear and begun to write, we step up to the plateau of frustration. Fear followed by frustration is the essence of writerly despair.

One reason writing is so frustrating is that after we've attended the courses, read the books, and gotten fired up to actually write, we hit the wall of working all alone, then sending what results to cold-eyed editors who couldn't care less about our state of mind. When our writing isn't as good as we hoped it would be (it never is), and editors seem to think our submissions aren't much good at all (they seldom do), how do we keep from succumbing to terminal despair?

Sometimes the only reason to keep writing is "just because." Or as a matter of faith; keeping the faith. "On some days," wrote novelist Gail Godwin in an essay about writing, "keeping faith means simply *staying there*, when more than anything else I want to get out of that room. It sometimes means going up *without hope* and *without energy* and simply acknowledging my barrenness and lighting my incense and turning on my computer. And, at the end of two or three hours, and *without hope* and *without energy*, I find that I have indeed written some sentences that wouldn't have been there if I hadn't gone up to write them. And—what is even more surprising—these sentences written without hope or energy often turn out to be just as good as the ones I wrote *with* hope and energy."

Before turning off your computer and turning on the television in moments of despair, reflect on the experience of authors such as Gail Godwin. Their situation was desperate but far from hopeless. Like yours, perhaps. You might want to consider how many writers have felt almost terminally discouraged but lived to write another day. As we'll see throughout this book, nearly every writer who appears to have it made was once on the brink of collapse.

This chapter began with the story of a struggling novice novelist named John. Here is the rest of his story.

John, as you may have guessed, is John Grisham, the most commercially successful author of modern times. Even as his agent was having trouble selling Grisham's second novel, studio scouts in Hollywood heard about it and began bidding furiously against each other to buy rights to this book. Paramount won, paying $600,000 for the privilege of making it into a movie. That piqued the interest of publishers (to put it mildly), and Doubleday offered Grisham $200,000 for *The Firm*. The rest, as we say, is history: book sales in the millions, multimillion-dollar advances, a mansion in Mississippi, an estate in Virginia. Grisham has since mused about what his life might have been like if he'd succumbed to despair in the midst of his fledgling efforts, as he almost did.

Few writers will ever enjoy John Grisham's success in the marketplace. But we all can learn from his example of fortitude in the face of anxiety, frustration, and despair. These constitute the sensibility of working writers everywhere, what I call AFD syndrome.

AFD Syndrome

I sit here religiously every morning—I sit down for eight hours every day—and the sitting down is all. In the course of that working day of 8 hours I write 3 sentences which I erase before leaving the table in despair. . . . Sometimes it takes all my resolution and power of self-control to refrain from butting my head against the wall.

Joseph Conrad

On those days or mornings when you feel worst, when you think everything is hopeless, that nothing will happen—sometimes the best things happen.

Walker Percy

AFD is the three-legged stool we sit on when writing. Its three legs are anxiety, frustration, and despair. *Anxiety* is what we feel when facing blank pages or computer screens because the moment of judgment has arrived. *Frustration* follows because the words we record on paper are rarely as good as the ones we meant to record. This leads to *despair*, the feeling that all is for naught. Together they become AFD syndrome, a state of mind whose separate elements can be hard to tell apart. Those who can't deal with this syndrome cannot write seriously. It's that simple.

You can't write in hopes that you'll be the exception: a writer of constant joy. This doesn't mean that joyful moments, even ecstatic ones, aren't part of the writing process. They are. But writers don't, and can't, write in hopes of achieving mere happiness. They're hunting for far bigger game. That's why AFD is their constant companion. Any undertaking of this scope will frighten, frustrate, and, on occasion, drive those who write to dark nights of despair.

That sounds like bad news. As we'll see, however, it isn't necessarily so.

Nerves Are Normal

In the same week that her twelfth Kinsey Millhone novel leaped to number one on the *New York Times* bestseller list, Sue Grafton addressed a group of fledgling writers. They were expecting confident words of wisdom from one of the most successful novelists of their time. What they got was a confession of how anxious writing made her. Grafton explained that whenever she sat down to write, an inner voice taunted her. "You're such a *putz*," this voice jeered, "you're gonna get that sentence wrong."

In *The Courage to Write* I focused on fear. The premise of that book was that anyone who presumes to put words on paper for others to read is subject to "page fright." If they aren't scared, they aren't writing (anything of consequence, that is). Now let's consider fear's menacing first cousin—anxiety—what our grandparents called *nerves*. Anxiety is more muted than fear as such, more ongoing, the nervousness we feel every time we sit down to write. Fear is a piercing wound, anxiety a throbbing toothache. One is the terror that everyone will see through us and hate us when they read what we've written, the other a shiver of concern that we just won't get the words right.

Anxiety goes with the writing territory. I've felt it. Sue Grafton has too. So has anyone who presumed to put words on paper for others to read. All writers tiptoe through a minefield of nerves on the way to their desk. "I cannot tell you the dread I have," said novelist Ethan Canin, using a word popular among authors when describing how it feels to approach blank pages. Gail Godwin wrote of the "outright *dreads*" that accompany her whenever she climbs the stairs to her study. "It's low dread every morning," agreed Joan Didion.

Feelings such as these leap off the pages of the posthumously published diaries and letters of prominent authors. John Cheever's journals are filled with anxiety, envy of other writers, and self-recrimination about the shortcomings of his own work. In one entry Cheever raved about Norman Mailer's *The Naked and the Dead*, then added, "Despaired, while reading it, of my own confined talents." A few years later the future Pulitzer Prize winner referred to "the contemptible smallness, the mediocrity" of his work. The year after that, he reminded himself, "Must avoid panic."

No matter how composed an author may appear at a book signing, when it comes to actually writing, aplomb is the exception, insecurity the norm. Even writers who appear to be cool, calm, and collected are usually quite the opposite inside. They may don a serene mask to go out in public, but at their desk those who record words on paper are consumed with inner doubts. Novelist Charles Baxter called feelings of inadequacy "the black-lung disease of writing." "Bracing self-confidence among writers is a rare commodity," Baxter added, "and often a sign of psychic instability." Those who deny this are bluffing, mostly. All writers get anxious, even those who are household names. "I never start a book without being terrified I won't finish it," admitted novelist Danielle Steel, "and I never finish a book without being terrified I won't start another."

In 1924, F. Scott Fitzgerald wrote his editor, Maxwell Perkins, to apologize for his delay in completing the novel that would become *The Great Gatsby*. "I'm doing the best I can," he explained. "I've gotten in dozens of bad habits that I'm trying to get rid of."

1. Laziness
2. Referring everything to [his wife] Zelda—a terrible habit, nothing ought to be referred to anybody until its finished.
3. Word consciousness—self doubt.

ect. ect. ect. ect. [Fitzgerald was a terrible speller.]

On the day of *Gatsby's* publication, Fitzgerald wrote Perkins, "I am overcome with fears and forebodings. . . . In fact all my confidence is gone."

Obviously experience, success, and public acclaim are no antidote to writing anxiety. Over time we just trade one form for another. Writing can't be done without anxiety. Nor should it be. Nerves are normal. One never enjoys nervousness, but it's integral to the writing process, perhaps even essential. Writers of all kinds learn to live with their nerves. They even come to depend on them. "Part of the investment a writer makes is an investment in anxiety," said novelist Martin Amis. "I don't think a novel could be any good at all if you weren't violently up and down about it."

Even though anxiety is a normal response to the act of writing, it is rarely faced head-on by teachers, editors, or even by writers themselves. They may not even be conscious of it. Anxiety is a master of disguise: laziness, procrastination, evasiveness, blocks, giving up altogether. Anxiety is the main reason that writers don't complete projects they start, can't put completed projects in the mail, write evasively, or don't write at all. ("Just some silly notion I had when I was a kid.") Another mask anxiety wears is one of arrogance. It's as true of snotty writers as of snotty people in general that their arrogance is a symptom of being scared to death—especially that others might realize how anxious they are.

Writing for public scrutiny must be anxiety-inducing for anyone with a gram of sensitivity, an ounce of self-doubt. Which is to say, everyone. (Which is one reason so many authors write under the influence, or a pseudonym.) Anyone who presumes to put words on paper for others to scrutinize is subject to nerves. How could they not be? Writing is a perilous proposition. This activity has more in common with fighting fires than, say, teaching English. Anxiety to a writer is like fire to a firefighter: an inevitable part of what they sign up for. It is also part of what makes this activity so compelling. Deep satisfaction comes from daring to do something we're not sure we can do. Anxiety follows. Those who write when anxious feel more pride than shame, and should. One thing that makes writing rewarding is the very fact that it *is* scary. If this weren't a nervous-making business, where would the satisfaction be? The challenge? The excitement?

Edgy writing holds our attention, and writing with an edge is most likely to come from writers on the edge. The better the writing, the more anxious the writer. The deeper they dig, the more alarmed they get. I can't write about *that*, can I? Only if you want to engage your reader. Anxiety accompanies the first true word we put on paper, and the last. We might even say that being anxious means we're actually writing something significant, something that could get us in trouble. If our writing doesn't make us anxious, there could be something seriously wrong.

Many writers are *more* nervous about committing words to paper than the average person. That's why they work at it so hard. They're determined not to let nerves lay them low. The prolific Norman Mailer said that his dozens of books were written in part to keep dread at bay. Nonwriters often assume that writers must be very dedicated because they spend so much time writing. That's true of some. For others it's just the opposite: they write without cease due to fear that taking a day away from their desk might mean they'd never return. Their productivity is a product, not a by-product, of insecurity. Stephen King has attributed his book-a-year output in part to trying to "outrun the self-doubt that's always waiting to settle in."

In this sense, anxiety is the flywheel of achievement. I find that the more anxious I feel, the more fully I focus on the task at hand. It's why I overresearch everything I write, and spend so much time rewriting—a first-rate antidote for nerves. *Antidote* is actually the wrong word. *Analgesic* is probably more accurate. There's no cure for writing anxiety. At best one comes to terms with feeling anxious and comes to understand how normal nerves are.

One could see this perspective as discouraging. I prefer to see it as *en*couraging. I'm not alone. Everyone is anxious and insecure about their writing, even published authors. They hacked through the jungle of their anxiety and lived to tell their tales. Maybe I can too. But how do I cope with the frustration that follows?

Frustration Happens

Long after her short stories were being compared favorably with Anton Chekhov's, Alice Munro said, "I have too little confidence, not the real confidence to be a writer." Munro traced this sense back to the period in her twenties and thirties when she tried to raise kids in the pre-Pampers era, emulate a housewife, work in her husband's bookstore near Vancouver, and write a little too. The reason Munro chose to write short stories rather than novels was that she could only work when her three daughters took naps. These stories were usually the result of several months' effort, "many changes, some false directions, much fiddling, and some despair." Munro sent many of her stories to magazines. Few were accepted. This resulted in what she called "a failure of confidence." Munro's output began to dwindle. The lament of a young Vancouver housewife Munro depicted in her story "Cortes Island" could have been her own:

> I bought a school notebook and tried to write—did write, pages that started off authoritatively and then went dry, so that I had to tear them up and twist them up in hard punishment and put them in the garbage can. I did this over and over again until I had only the notebook cover left. Then I bought another notebook and started the whole process once more. The same cycle—excitement and despair, excitement and despair. It was like having a secret pregnancy and miscarriage every week.

Only the support (both financial and emotional) of a sympathetic husband and a few colleagues kept Munro writing. Her first collection—*Dance of the Happy Shades*—published when she was thirty-seven, took two decades to complete.

Munro's is a textbook case of frustration transcended. It is anything but untypical. Even when we face down our anxiety enough to keep recording words on paper, we're then faced with exasperation when all doesn't go as we'd planned. The words we record are seldom as good as we hoped they'd be. People we care about resent the time and attention we give our writing. Editors don't give that writing enough of their time and attention. Even if they buy our work, a multitude of aggravations are part of the publishing process.

Writing seriously means reaching for a brass ring that can never be seized. Frustration—the gulf between aspiration and results—accompanies any attempt to write seriously. "I've always felt I've never done well," said Nobel laureate Isaac Bash-evis Singer in his eighth decade. "I've always felt I should have done better. It was true when I was 30. It is true at 81." How could it be otherwise? Whenever you're onto something this big, you are bound to get frustrated. That's one way you know you're engaged in a challenging pursuit. The only people whose life's work doesn't exasperate them are those who have chosen modest goals.

There is a way to reduce frustration, of course: keep your aspirations low. The most serene writers I know don't take themselves, or their work, very seriously. They dash things off, rewrite little. A friend of mine once spent six weeks on a work of nonfiction that eventually got published. My friend said that this had been among the happiest six weeks of his life. He looked forward to many books to come. That was over two decades ago. He hasn't published a book since.

If you find that writing comes easily to you, you might want to examine why this is so. There could be a problem. Philip Roth said, "Fluency can be a sign that nothing is happening; fluency can actually be my signal to stop, while being in the dark from sentence to sentence is what convinces me to go on."

A truism among writers is that the better their writing, the harder it is to do. A continually requoted thought about their craft is Thomas Mann's observation that the writer is someone for whom writing is harder than it is for other people. One author went so far as to say we should always be writing the story we *can't*. That's almost like saying we should try to leap our way to the moon. If we take this advice, frustration is bound to follow.

It's no coincidence that some of our best writers experienced profound frustration along the way. Any writer with high standards gets frustrated. Frustration is a sign of seriousness; an indication that your reach is exceeding your grasp. That's why feeling discouraged is not necessarily a bad thing. It could mean you're on the right path.

That was how Maxwell Perkins saw it. The fabled Scribner editor was renowned for his patience with discouraged writers. One in particular, the novelist Nancy Hale, worked in a state of perpetual gloom and constant blockage. Perkins sympathized. "Writing a novel is a very hard thing to do . . . ," he wrote her, "and if you get discouraged it is not a bad sign but a good one. If you think you are not doing it well, you are thinking the way real novelists do. I never knew one who did not feel greatly discouraged at times, and some get desperate, and I have always found that to be a good symptom." In a subsequent letter, Perkins struck a similar chord. "I would be much more concerned if you did not have to go through periods of despair and anxiety and dissatisfaction," he told Hale. "It is true that a good many novelists do not, but I think the best ones truly do, and I do not see how it could be otherwise. . . . The struggle is part of the process."

In other words, if you are not discouraged about your writing on a regular basis, you may not be trying hard enough. Any challenging pursuit will encounter frequent patches of frustration. Writing is nothing if not challenging.

Perhaps that's as it ought to be. If writing were less aggravating, the field would be even more crowded than it is now. If we're to do this job, we must muddle through, slog through swamps of frustration. You can never conquer frustration. You can learn how to put up with this feeling and not let it keep you from doing the writing you want to do. Working writers have the highest regard for their frustration. They know it's a sign that they're still reaching for the brass ring. Theodore Roethke thought that the most important thing for a poet like him to have was not inspiration but "the right kind of frustration."

Tolerance for frustration gauges a writer's commitment, and capacity for growth. From that tolerance comes the ability to have a literary vocation, not just a sometime hobby. One danger, however, is that the common cold of frustration can escalate into the pneumonia of despair.

Before Drinking Hemlock

After one too many publishers rejected his novel, John Kennedy Toole attached a hose to his car's tailpipe, ran this hose through its front window, sat in the driver's seat, and turned on the ignition. He was thirty-one. The author's mother was more persistent. Thelma Toole kept submitting her late son's manuscript, with no better results. Finally, Mrs. Toole called Walker Percy. Her son's book was *great*, she assured him. Would he read the manuscript? Against his better judgment, the novelist said he would. Percy was sure he'd only have to read a few paragraphs to justify returning the smudged carbon copy. He was wrong. Percy later recalled that Toole's writing made him "gape, grin, laugh out loud, shake my head in wonderment." On Percy's recommendation, the Louisiana State University Press finally published *A Confederacy of Dunces*. Twelve years after he committed suicide, Toole's novel won the Pulitzer Prize for fiction. To date it has sold well over 1 million copies.

Desperation defeats far more aspiring writers than lack of ability. What they don't realize is that desperation is the writers' norm, serenity the exception. Periods of despair are as inevitable as high tides in the ocean. This is true whether they've been writing for four months or four decades. Despair is not just an affliction of neophytes. It is part of every writer's job description.

After noting how desperate the prolific H. L. Mencken often felt, Mencken's biographer, William Manchester, observed, "That is an aspect of writing which writers would rather not explore. Theirs is, quite simply, a desperate business."

During the early 1850s, Gustave Flaubert kept up a steady correspondence with the poet Louise Colet. These letters—dutifully dated—constituted a litany of how frustrated, discouraged, and desperate Flaubert often felt.

2 1 52 Bad week. Work didn't go. I had reached a point where I didn't know what to say. It was all shadings and refinements; I was completely in the dark: it is very difficult to clarify by means of words what is still obscure in your thoughts. I made outlines, spoiled a lot of paper, floundered and fumbled.

4 24 52 You speak of your discouragement. If you could see mine! . . . Sometimes, when I am empty, when words don't come, when I find I haven't written a single sentence after scribbling whole pages, I collapse on my couch and lie there dazed, bogged in a swamp of despair. . . .

4 7 54 What a struggle it has been! My God, what a struggle! Such drudgery! Such discouragement!

The result, of course, was *Madame Bovary.*

The fact that writers work alone magnifies their sense of desperation. Because this is such an isolated activity, those who write find it easy to succumb to despair. Just when they need encouragement most, there's no one around to give it. Sitting day after day with only a keyboard and telephone for company is especially hard if you're in any way a social animal. For those used to the company—good or bad, but company—of coworkers, spending day after day in isolation can be unnerving. No one is around to offer a goose or a kiss to the writer at work. "He works in a room alone," wrote H. L. Mencken of himself and his colleagues. "Every jangle of the telephone cuts him like a knife; every entrance of a visitor blows him up. . . . His every physical sensation is enormously magnified. A cold in the head rides him like a witch. A split fingernail hurts worse than a laparotomy. The smart of a too-close shave burns like a prairie fire. A typewriter that bucks is worse than a band of music. The far-away wail of a child is the howling of a fiend. A rattling radiator is a battery of artillery."

Mencken exaggerated, but not much. Far more of my colleagues have been driven back to newspaper offices or public relations firms by the harrowing isolation of writing for a living than by its financial suspense. The reason so many gifted writers end up on scriptwriting teams has as much to do with the company as the cash. Those who generate their own writing must come to terms with themselves. One friend of mine left steady employment as a journalist to write a book. Later, he left that calling to become an on-air television reporter. When I asked if he thought he'd ever write another book, my friend gave me a quizzical look. "I don't know," he said, shaking his head.

Why not?

He smiled enigmatically and said, "I'm not sure I enjoy my own company that much."

To be a writer, one must be willing to put up with the psychic demands of actually *writing*. Authors on talk shows emphasize their thrilling moments of triumph, not the months and years of monotony and malaise that preceded those moments. Movies about writers seldom succeed because their actual life is so much less interesting than fictionalized versions. As Virginia Woolf observed, the sense of creativity that "bubbles so pleasantly in the beginning of a new book" always subsides. Then a new, steadier type of energy is called for. Toward the end, she concluded, "determination not to give in . . . keep one at it more than anything."

Malaise is an occupational hazard of being a determined writer. This is true of writing sessions and writing careers. Consider the career of Cynthia Ozick. After writing for nearly half a century, Ozick has become a literary luminary, nearly a household name. Yet, for the better part of two decades, she wrote in obscurity and submitted her writing with nary a nibble from editors. Like Alice Munro, Ozick nearly faltered during desperate years in her twenties and thirties when some of the best agents and editors in New York returned her work on a regular basis. One prominent editor rejected an early version of Ozick's novel *Trust* with such a scathing letter that for several months she was too demoralized to write. After finally completing *Trust* in her late thirties, Ozick went to the *New York Review of Books* in search of a reviewing assignment. Years later she could still recall standing in the open door of that magazine's office and being dismissed by the receptionist. "I was not even invited across the doorsill," said Ozick. That same day she had an essay rejected by *Commentary*. The author's confidence in herself nearly evaporated, and only her belief in capital-*L Literature* sustained Ozick during this long period of—in her words— "humiliation, of total shame and defeat."

Nonwriters might be forgiven for wondering why writers prolong the agony. Why don't they just drink their hemlock and get it over with? Well? Why don't we?

For one thing, as Alice Munro and Cynthia Ozick demonstrated, it is possible to write through AFD, to get beyond one's anxiety, frustration, even one's despair. Recall the aspiring writer in Munro's "Cortes Island" whose cycles of life consisted of "excitement and despair, excitement and despair." Writing is not so much a depressive as a manic-depressive business, both a downer and an upper. All writers have good days and bad days. When you are recording words on paper, it's hard not to ride an emotional roller coaster. The same writers who one day say nothing depresses them more than writing the next day say nothing is more thrilling. Lows may be lower for writers, but highs are higher. On Easter day in 1853, Flaubert wrote Louise Colet, "I sometimes have moments of bitterness that make me almost scream with rage (so acutely do I feel my own impotence and weakness). I have others when I can scarcely contain myself for joy."

Something that continually surprises writers is how little the quality of their mood has to do with the quality of their writing. The writing they do when joyful may not survive a second draft. Words recorded at desperate moments aren't necessarily bad ones. Writers sometimes retrieve a crumpled piece of paper they'd thrown on the floor in despair the day before, smooth it out, read the contents, and to their surprise, find a decent piece of work.

One's mood when writing is no barometer of the results. Some writers even find an inverse correlation between the state of their mind and the quality of their work. William Gass often got so tense while writing that he left his desk and paced about the house. Because writing was hard on his stomach, Gass chewed lots of pills to keep his ulcer in check. Not that this detracted from his output. To the contrary, said Gass, "When my work is going well, I am usually sort of sick."

It is only when I begin to feel out of sorts while writing that I know I'm getting serious. How I feel when I begin to write has little to do with how I feel by the end. The words I record on paper when down can't be distinguished from the ones I write when up. Sometimes they're even better. Some of our best writing grows out of our worst times. Using Churchill's term for depression, Robertson Davies observed that even though every writer he knew was well acquainted with the Black Dog, somehow they wrote anyway, and "the passages written when the Black Dog was at his most malignant may be the best."

Dark, downhearted days can be a sign that something important is struggling to emerge from the caverns of our psyches. Work we produce on those days may prove to be very good work indeed. Even though AFD syndrome can't be "conquered," it can become a first-rate source of material. The depression that J. K. Rowling suffered while writing her first Harry Potter book inspired her to create the "Dementors," who vacuum out happy memories, leaving only desperate ones. Fiction writers like Rowling who use their own despair to inform characters have found a powerful writing tool. After all, other people's misfortune is usually more interesting to read about than their good fortune. Bad days provide good grist for writing mills. The power of Anne Sexton's poetry owed far more to her troubled postgraduate life than her happy days as a high school cheerleader. It was his many frustrations that led thirty-eight-year-old Marcel Proust to pour out his sense of failure in *Remembrance of Things Past*. Would readers have been as interested in a contented Proust?

· 3 ·

Dealing with Discouragers

"Please," he said. "Have pity on me. I've spent the whole day trying to dodge one of my mother's negative comments after another. 'Wherever did you get the odd idea that you could write a book?' is my personal favorite. As far as I'm concerned, that was the topper on the cake."

J. A. Jance, *Devil's Claw*

The great pleasure in life is doing what people say you cannot do.

Walter Bagehot

In an ideal world, frustrated writers would receive the soothing balm of encouraging words from all family members, every friend, most colleagues, and people they'd just met at a dinner party. That world doesn't exist. Unlike Gene Autry's home on the range, writing is *not* the place where discouraging words are seldom heard. All writers hear many of them: from teachers, counselors, coworkers, spouses, and their aunt Edna in Des Moines. This gauntlet of *discouragers* is one that must be run by anyone who wishes to write. Once we realize where they are coming from, however, discouragers lose their sting. Discouragers can be dispatched by understanding their motives and by putting them to work as goads.

Discouragers

Were you ever advised to forget about writing? If so, you have lots of company. Teachers are sometimes the source of this advice. Patricia MacLachlan (*Sarah, Plain and Tall*) was warned by a high school teacher that she should seek another profession because writing wouldn't be it. At Ohio University, a guidance counselor advised Erma Bombeck to forget about writing. In another part of the state, an Ohio State University professor told Harlan Ellison that he had no writing talent. By legend, Ellison sent this professor a copy of every one of the dozens of novels he proceeded to publish after dropping out from OSU.

A striking number of well-known writers were told they couldn't write (usually by someone who never enjoyed a fraction of their literary success). Such discouragers ply their trade with vigor, imagination, and enthusiasm. Some are as subtle as a rattlesnake. When Mavis Gallant told the cultural attaché at a Canadian embassy that she was a writer, he asked, "Yes, but what do you *really* do?" Others are passive-aggressive. F. Scott Fitzgerald recalled that when he told relatives and friends in St. Paul that he'd quit his job as an advertising man in New York to return home and write a novel, they "nodded politely, changed the subject and spoke of me very gently."

Aspiring writers are an easy target for wisecracks, chiding, snickers, ridicule, and gape-jawed disbelief. "Don't quit your day job!" is the most popular response, usually accompanied by a condescending chuckle. That's why literary aspirants so often tell others they're apprentice plumbers or medical students. Once they reveal their actual intention, they're fair game. They've been flushed out. Laughter ensues. "There are a lot of people out there who'll be damned if they let you get away with it, you jumped-up smarty-pants," said Margaret Atwood.

But I don't think amusement is what's really being expressed. The laughter is too nervous. It's a cover-up. The underlying motives of discouragers are complicated and usually have more to do with the debunker than the writer. Before abiding by someone's discouraging words, consider what they stand to gain by dissuading you from writing.

Projectors

After she published a poetry collection at the age of twenty-six, Margaret Atwood's brother sent her a complimentary note. "Congratulations on publishing your first book of poetry," he wrote. "I used to do that kind of thing myself when I was younger." This is a classic double message. In the guise of praise it is actually an attempt to undercut someone doing something one used to do, might like to be doing still, and would rather someone else not be doing—especially a sibling.

Writers bear the burden of being a magnet for issues of those who would keep them earthbound. They trigger inner anxieties of those with frustrations of their own. "You carry upon your shoulders the weight of other people's projections," suggested Atwood, "of their fears and fantasies and anxieties and superstitions."

Like Atwood's own brother, relatives and friends are among the worst discouragers. But they usually have their own drama in production in which you play only a small role. Think of them as *projectors*. Friends may fear that you'll succeed and no longer be their friend. They may be worried that you might write about them, or—worse yet—that you won't. Parents and other relatives are routinely anxious about family beans being spilled. Edward Hoagland's corporate lawyer father was concerned that his son's career as an essayist would damage their social standing. Long after she'd achieved literary renown,

Edith Wharton's parents were so embarrassed by her choice of career that they wouldn't even discuss it. Scott Turow was discouraged from becoming a writer by a mother who'd wanted to become one herself.

Steve Martin found himself on the horns of a similar dilemma, one he was not aware of until relatively late in life. Throughout his career as a comedian-actor-director-writer, Martin felt belittled by his realtor father. Martin *père* once went so far as to give his son a bad review in a newsletter for real estate agents. It turned out that Glenn Martin was a failed thespian who had turned to selling property only after his dream of becoming an actor was tucked tightly away in a trunk. On his deathbed Steve Martin's father finally admitted, "You did everything I always wanted to do."

This can be a powerful motivation for discouraging a child from embarking on a creative career such as writing: not wanting that child to do something a parent could not. If motives were on the surface, we would probably be amazed by how many discouragers—including parents—are (or were) closet writers themselves. Most of us have such aspirations. Something all published writers quickly discover is how many people they meet "plan to do some writing one of these days." One poll found that 81 percent of a representative American sample said they'd like to write a book. Eighty-one percent! That group undoubtedly includes many of those who try to discourage others from doing what they wish they would do themselves.

Enviers

Ann Beattie found that the longer she wrote and the larger her reputation grew, the more complicated were responses from others. In Beattie's words, "People's anxiety, or simply their desire, has also increased exponentially. I am doing what they

want to do. I am—or Mavis Gallant is, or Alice Munro is—
who they want to be."

For better and worse, becoming a writer means becoming
the surrogate risk taker for many others. But the flattery implied
or even stated in that status is usually laced with defensiveness
("I would've done what you're doing except that . . ."). Then a
litany of excuses like those we'll consider in the next chapter
is recited (no time; no money; kids to raise; dinner to make;
etc.). Implicit in this defensiveness is the discouragers' prayer
that you will fail and confirm their wisdom in not staying the
course.

That is why, like so many of my colleagues, I seldom vol-
unteer what I do for a living. Doing so strikes too many ambivalent chords in too many listeners: surprise, awe, disbelief, envy,
resentment, and antagonism (to mention just a few). Like acting, or playing a professional sport, writing is a Peter Pan profession: not quite grown-up. It's hard to assimilate that someone
you're talking to actually does this for a living (or tries to), and
harder yet to cope with the mixed feelings this ignites—not
just about writing but about any unpursued dream of one's
own. Such ambivalence is central to those who would discourage. Envy is the fuel driving their engine. "I divide mankind
into two categories," wrote Chekhov, "writers and enviers! The
former write, and the latter die of jealousy and spend all their
time plotting and scheming against them."

The most discouraging words invariably come from enviers who have put their youthful ambitions in a hope chest.
Those who have renounced their own dreams routinely belit-
tle those who haven't. *"You'll never be a writer"* could be a
sincere assessment of your prospects. Or it could simply be a
way to recruit new members into the fraternity of the terminally discouraged. The persistence of a colleague who is
pursuing an out-of-the-ordinary dream such as writing is like

a beacon illuminating the timidity of dream pursuit dropouts. Encouraging you to renounce your aspirations will confirm detractors' wisdom in renouncing their own.

A friend of mine who took a flyer on freelance writing told
me that many colleagues back at her former office were sca-
thingly skeptical about her new career, and not hesitant to let
her know. "Other people often *need* you to fail," concluded my
friend, a psychologist, "to justify their own fears and inertia."

The longer you write, the more you will remind others of
their unpursued dreams. If you stay with it, you'll be a constant
reminder of the towel they've thrown in. If they can bully you
into tossing in your own towel, they'll feel vindicated for throwing in their own. If you can keep your towel firmly in hand,
however, the needling of discouragers not only can be endured
but can become a powerful source of motivation.

Goads

A poet named Julia Levine once told me about the early obstacles that built a foundation for her later success. In college, a
creative writing teacher had advised Levine to forget about
becoming a poet. "This is crap," she recalled him saying about
one of her poems. "You've got no talent." His devastating
assessment made Levine stop writing for a time. Then she
became a closet poet, showing her work to no one. Eventually,
Levine began sending poems to magazines. Many were published, and some won awards. So much for her professor's
assessment. I told the poet that she should be grateful for such
a terrific nemesis. For one thing, he steered her into a primary
career as a clinical psychologist working with disturbed children. This gave Levine a treasure chest of material to transform
into poems. More important, debunking teachers like hers gives

writers like Levine a goad; someone to *show* that they can do what he thought they couldn't.

Writers would be lost without such energizers. They are defiant people. They must be, to endure and transcend all the discouraging words thrown their way. A key target of writers' defiance is any teacher, colleague, agent, or editor who said they couldn't make it. Rather than be discouraged by such doubters, they convert them into goads. They're determined to send these debunkers a message. Their writing is that message.

Novelist Ann Patchett said she became a writer because writing was so hard for her in school and earned her such opprobrium from teachers. One nun in particular made Patchett feel like a dunce. "I write for her," she said after publishing three novels. "Even as a child I wanted to write for revenge, to show them all, but especially this particular nun, that I had been misjudged." If she'd encountered a more supportive teacher, Patchett has wondered, would she have been so determined to write?

Don't underestimate the value of such provocateurs. They can be the source not only of great energy but of wonderful material as well. Cynthia Ozick's novel *The Laughter of Akiva* savaged teachers like the ones who taught her at P.S. 71 in the Bronx "who hurt me, who made me believe I was stupid and inferior." Kevin Williamson's movie *Teaching Mrs. Tingle* had a similar genesis. According to Williamson, a high school English teacher once told him, "Yours is a voice that shouldn't be heard." He was devastated enough by this put-down to avoid writing for more than a decade. After regaining his voice and his confidence, Williamson became a screenwriter who enjoyed great success with movies such as *Scream* and the television series *Dawson's Creek*. Then he wrote and directed *Teaching Mrs. Tingle*, in which he satirized a teacher like the one who'd consigned his writing to silence.

Working writers thrive on put-downs. They cultivate nemeses, brood about grievances, fan the flames of their anger. To them, doubters, injustice, and supercilious criticism are all great motivators. Sue Grafton's career as a mystery writer began as an effort to prove discouragers wrong. In her case the discouragers were Hollywood producers who, when she was writing screenplays, told Grafton she was good at characterization but not at plot. Grafton knew that plot was everything in mystery novels, so she began writing them, primarily as a way to make those producers eat their words. "And I did just that," she concluded.

One reason successful writers carry on in the face of devastating assessments of their prospects is that they're so determined to prove wrong anyone who tried to push them off the path. Far from being discouraged, they find such efforts one more reason to stay the course. Writers with points to make, doubters to show, detractors to prove wrong, don't give up easily. How could they? Giving up would give skeptics the satisfaction of seeming to be right. Turning away from writing would confirm negative predictions about their prospects.

Having succeeded in doing what they were told couldn't be done, published writers can be magnanimous to those who tried to discourage them. But they don't forget their names. Successful people in all fields routinely point to some foil in their past, a Cassandra who told them not to pursue their dream and instead became an inspiration for doing so. In a wonderful essay on his own failure and sense of despair, Charles Baxter depicted an agent named "Julie" whose response to a novel he sent her was, "I hate it." This novel was subsequently published, followed by others. "Thank you, Julie, wherever you are, for your cruelty to me," wrote Baxter. "Couldn't have done it without you."

A determination to put detractors in their place characterizes successful writers no less than it does professional athletes who were cut by high school coaches, and actors who got cast as trees in the sixth-grade play. Those with long lists of doubters to prove wrong are among the most determined writers of all. Names on this list become first-rate motivators. Larry L. King (*The Best Little Whorehouse in Texas*) said about his years of rejection early in his career, "Each rejection . . . seemed to spur me onward with a grimmer determination to prove the bastards wrong." This being the case, King found that his maiden book contract nearly did him in. For weeks after receiving his first check as a Professional Writer, King found himself staring at blank pages without being able to put any words on them.

As one writer after another has discovered, success can be a serious demotivator. After her novel *Kinflicks* did so well, Lisa Alther's career stalled. One reason was the positive light in which she was now regarded. Part of her motivation in writing that first novel, Alther conceded, had been thinking, "Well, I'll show you"—the "you" being all those editors who had rejected her early work. Now she had to deal with editors who asked, "When will you have your next story?" instead of, "Why are you darkening my doorway?" The result, in Alther's words, was "one of your motives is taken away."

The Ashes of Success

In 1929—the year Thomas Wolfe's *Look Homeward Angel*, Ernest Hemingway's *A Farewell to Arms*, and William Faulkner's *The Sound and the Fury* were published—novelist Julia M. Peterkin won the Pulitzer Prize for letters for her novel *Scarlet Sister Mary*.

Reading lists of writing awards is an eye-opener. They are routinely given to writers whose work sinks from view within a few decades, even a few years. Few are authors whose work, or reputation, outlive their moment of glory. Pulitzer Prize winners for fiction during the past few decades have included: Margaret Ayer Barnes, T. S. Stribling, Caroline Miller, Josephine Johnson, Harold Davis, Ellen Glasgow, Martin Flavin, and Robert Lewis Taylor.

Writers who win major literary prizes routinely struggle to produce anything comparable to the work that won them the prize. Authors awarded Nobels are really in the soup (as John Steinbeck fretted, with reason; his own productive life did not survive his Nobel prize). Albert Camus suffered crippling writer's block after winning his Nobel. One reason could be that feeling accepted, feeling *popular,* as it were, deprives them of a primary energy source. Perhaps Nobels and Pulitzers and Bookers are too effective an antidote to bile.

The same thing might be said of too-early success. It's a truism among writers that early flashes seldom escape the pan. We hear a lot about the many twenty-somethings (or younger) who command big advances and generate lots of buzz—especially among their agemates in the media. Younger writers have the virtues of energy, hipness, tight skin, and thick heads of hair. But they suffer downsides, too, including (as we'll see in the next chapter) timidity. Many burn out early. The history of publishing is littered with writers of great promise who published a book or two in their twenties, then disappeared. Most of those who publish one novel never publish another. Many simply can't shoulder the burden of what Thomas Wolfe called "the terrible, soul-shaking, heart-rending barrier of the accursed second book."

When he reviewed the many gifted young writers whose work he'd published in *New American Review* over a decade's time, the magazine's founder and editor, Theodore Solotaroff, was dismayed to note how few had ever been heard from again. A quarter or so had gone on to reasonably successful literary careers, another quarter to marginal ones. Half had vanished altogether (literarily speaking). Solotaroff wondered if those writers might not have been better off waiting, honing their skills, their nerve, and their fortitude. He believed that one of the worst things that could happen to gifted young writers was to win too much acclaim too young and bypass the rejection-frustration-despair syndrome that would prepare them for the long haul of a literary career. Solotaroff was concerned that those early-success writers might never learn how to convert "diffuse anger and disappointment into deliberate and durable aggression, the writer's main source of energy."

This perspective suggests that when it comes to reasons not to write, we're dealing with more than external discouragers. Even more insidious than discouragement from without is that from within: the apparently plausible reasons we all come up with to avoid writing. Since you are reading this book, I assume you want to write. But you may feel there are compelling reasons why you can't, or why you are stalled. Let's examine the most common ones and see how well these reasons hold up.

· 4 ·

Exorcising Excuses

I'm writing a second novel, which is going slowly because I wake up in the morning anxious, instead, to clean my house.

protagonist in Carol Shields's *Unless*

Where do you come up with your rationalizations for not writing?

younger woman to older man, *New Yorker* cartoon

When Mary Higgins Clark was thirty-six, her husband died of a heart attack. Clark was left with five young children to raise, a mortgage to pay, and no job. She found work producing radio scripts and wrote an occasional short story on the side. Writing from five to seven in the morning, before getting her kids off to school, Clark spent three years working on a biography of George Washington called *Aspire to the Heavens*. This book was published, but sank without a trace. Clark then spent three more years writing a suspense novel called *Where Are the Children?* After it had been rejected by two other publishers, Simon & Schuster bought Clark's novel for a $3,000 advance. In the decades after *Where Are the Children?* was published, Mary Higgins Clark became one of the most commercially successful authors of all time.

Clark has always said that—financial considerations aside—

not writing was never an option for her. She was driven. This being the case, Clark made time to write. She had to. "I'm not happy if I'm not writing," the novelist explained. Needless to say, she has little patience with nonwriting aspiring writers. In Clark's opinion they've succumbed to what she calls "As soon as" syndrome. *As soon as: the kids are grown, the dog dies, I leave my husband, I get a better computer or a pristine place to write.* "I say," said Clark, "nope, it ain't gonna happen with that attitude."

Like Clark and most working writers, I'm impressed by how many people tell me they plan to do some writing; someday. They just don't seem to get around to it. We all have terrific excuses not to write, valid ones, ones that no one would fault us for not abiding. Except, once one set of reasons is resolved—once the kids are grown, the dog's dead, and the spouse is history—another set usually takes its place. Courses need to be taken, the garage cleared out, calls made, teams coached, recipes transferred to one's computer.

Not writing is one of the great excuse-generators of all time. Here are the top six.

1) I Don't Have Enough Time

Ann Patchett once observed that whenever she began a novel, her apartment became remarkably clean. An amazing number of long-neglected chores cry out to be tended to in writers' homes once the prospect of writing looms. "I remember so clearly," a sometime writer once told me, "that the absolutely most loathsome tasks of my household (sorting out closets and cleaning the oven) suddenly took on tremendous appeal approximately ten minutes after I sat down at my typewriter and stared at a blank page."

Parents, of course, can make a compelling case for not writing. *You don't expect me to raise kids and write too, do you?* Many have. Ursula LeGuin wrote science fiction throughout her children's infancy, after she'd put them to bed. Stephen King produced *Salem's Lot* after he'd finished teaching high school English and his kids were asleep, using a portable typewriter perched on a child's desk that was crammed into the furnace room of his mobile home. James Baldwin grew so accustomed to writing after his siblings were in bed and he'd finished his multiple day jobs that he became a confirmed nocturnal writer.

Carol Shields wrote poetry in odd bits of time she stole away from diapering and nursing the five children she bore in a decade's time. Once they began school, Shields began a novel, writing for an hour in the late morning before her kids came home for lunch, and perhaps a bit more in the midafternoon before they came home for good, going over the two pages she'd written in the morning. Occasionally, if she hadn't been able to meet her two-page quota during the day, the Canadian novelist would take a yellow pad to bed with her and write some more before she went to sleep. Nine months of two-page-a-day writing resulted in her first novel: *Small Ceremonies*. Shields later observed that she never wrote this quickly again, or in such an organized way. Having to work around her family duties made Shields more efficient with her time, more tightly scheduled. This resulted in a steady output of successors, including *The Stone Diaries*. "It's funny," Shields told National Public Radio's Terry Gross several years after she won a Pulitzer Prize for that novel, "because now I have the whole day and my output is no more than it was then."

The very assumption that lots of free time is an asset for writers may be questionable. In some ways part-timers have an edge. Busy people organize their schedules more carefully and make better use of the few hours they do have to write. Anthony Trollope attributed his prolific output to the simple fact that having a day job (as a post office official) forced him to hyperorganize his after-hours writing sessions. Trollope doubted that he'd have produced any more with unlimited time to write. He might even have produced less. This is a surprising discovery among writers who have seen both sides. Sue Grafton said she made best use of her time while raising two children and working full-time, writing on the side. She got more done because her time was so compressed. Once Grafton's kids were grown and she quit her job to write full-time, it proved easy to squander an embarrassment of riches. "Now I can write all day long and I can't get anything done," said Grafton after she became an affluent empty-nester. "So I think a full-time job is a blessing."

Bear in mind that John Grisham wrote his first two novels while lawyering full-time, serving in the Mississippi state legislature, helping raise his son, and teaching Sunday school. Frank Yerby began the first of dozens of novels while working as a quality control inspector at a Long Island aircraft factory during World War II. Agatha Christie produced a dozen novels in half that number of years while working full-time in a hospital during that war. Margaret Edson wrote the Pulitzer Prize–winning play *Wit* when she got off work at a bicycle shop. Christopher Paul Curtis began the career that led to winning the American Library Association's Newbery Medal (for best children's book of the year) during breaks while working on the assembly line at the Fisher Body Plant No. 1 in Flint, Michigan. Scott Turow wrote *Presumed Innocent* in spiral notebooks during his daily half-hour train commute to work as a lawyer in Chicago. After bell hooks began writing essays while working eight hours a day at the phone company, a friend observed, "It is amazing how much writing we black women can produce even when we are worried sick about finances and job pressures."

These writers took seriously the advice not to quit their day jobs, and even found it to their advantage. In addition to having to schedule time effectively, writers with day jobs have access to a rich, ongoing source of material. Those with vocations other than writing have something to write *about*. Certainly, that's been the experience of Scott Turow and the many lawyer-colleagues who subsequently wrote their own novels, including John Grisham, Steve Martini, and Lisa Scottoline. (These days, *lawyer* and *aspiring author* seem almost oxymoronic.) Grisham thought one reason so many lawyers were becoming writers was that with front-row seats to observe gripping, seamy characters and events, their plots virtually wrote themselves. William Carlos Williams didn't give up the practice of medicine after becoming a successful poet, because he found it kept him connected to life at large and inspired some of his best poems. Practicing medicine, Williams found, let him peer "into the secret gardens of the self." Other doctor-authors— Anton Chekhov, Somerset Maugham, Richard Seltzer, Sherwin Nuland—found the same thing. "Medicine is my lawful wife and literature is my mistress," Chekhov wrote his publisher. "When I get tired of one, I spend the night with the other. Though it's disorderly, it's not so dull and besides, neither loses anything through my infidelity."

To finish calling the roll of distinguished writers with day jobs: Franz Kafka was a clerk, Herman Melville a customs official, Primo Levi an industrial chemist. T. S. Eliot worked in a bank before he became an editor. Throughout his career as a librarian, Philip Larkin wrote most of his poems after work. When the prospect of early retirement loomed, the librarian took a pass. Unlimited free time might be wonderful, he thought, for about two days. After that, full-time writing would be accompanied by "the *boredom*, the *depression*. Listening to the morning service on the BBC. Counting the minutes till drink time. Going out to the shops and realizing you're just one silly sod among thousands." For all of that, Larkin did sometimes wonder what he might have been able to accomplish as a full-time writer with a fresh mind after a good night's sleep.

Perhaps not as much. Another advantage enjoyed by writers with day jobs is that exhaustion can erode inhibitions, help defeat the censors that always lurk about as we try to write. Resisting inner censorship is a key challenge for any writer. Fatigue can be a valuable ally in this struggle. This was what Debra Rienstra discovered. Rienstra was so sleep-deprived while producing her memoir, *Great with Child*, that she could not fully remember writing this book. It was done in exhausted fifteen- to sixty-minute stretches while the poet was pregnant with her third child, after the other two had gone to bed. Her fatigue gave the manuscript rawness and candor, Rienstra thought, because she didn't have her "editorial defenses up."

2) I'm Not Talented Enough

Few writers are. That doesn't keep them from writing. Here's what some have had to say on this subject:

> Do I have the talent to compare with our modern Russian writers? Decidedly not.
>
> LEO TOLSTOY

> I have never been so conscious of how little talent is vouchsafed me for expressing ideas in words.
>
> GUSTAVE FLAUBERT

I have no talent. It's just the question of working, of being
willing to put in the time.

GRAHAM GREENE

I don't think I was born with any talent.

LARRY BROWN

I don't think of myself as a naturally gifted writer.

JOSEPH HELLER

Natural gifts alone are no guarantee of the will to write, to
say nothing of the audacity and the persistence. Productive
writers don't need talent so much as determination. Will matters more than skill. I've seen far more would-be writers scuttled
by indolence and short attention spans than by lack of ability.
Regular work habits and high tolerance for tedium characterize
working writers. The ranks of aspirants who have deserted this
battle include battalions of the gifted. Those who stay to fight
another day tend to be more tenacious than talented. Successful
figures of all kinds know many others with more aptitude than
they, but few who are more determined.

George Garrett once observed that the honor roll of published authors included both gifted writers and ones without
much talent at all. But, added the novelist-teacher, "I defy you
to tell which are which." Willingness to stay with the hard work
of revision was what leveled the playing field, Garrett thought,
and allowed even writers of modest gifts to publish their work.

Writing teachers such as Garrett routinely note that their
most talented students are rarely the most productive ones.
Such teachers seldom see the bylines of their best graduates.
The names they do see in print are more likely to be ones of
quiet students in the back row. Those who wowed their classmates with dazzling metaphors and deft characterization usually
vanish. "In every writing class I've been in," noted Iowa Writ-

ers' Workshop graduate Bonnie Friedman in *Writing Past Dark*, "there was a brilliant student, a student whose words flung out in morning glories and birds-of-paradise on the page, and who left the rest of us gaping when he or she was done reading, inspired and even thankful. Almost every single one of those writers has disappeared!"

A writer with prospects can hardly be devoid of talent. But it doesn't take as much natural ability as one might think to become productive. In all manner of pursuits there's a tendency to overestimate brilliance and underestimate persistence. Talent is common. Determination is rare. A manager of musicians, who began his career thinking that natural gifts accounted for at least half of a successful musical career, in time reduced that proportion to a mere 20 percent. (John Berryman thought talent contributed to good poetry in the same proportion: 20 percent.) Research on music students has determined that achievement is correlated far more with number of hours practiced than with natural gifts. In fact, studies of those who excel in many fields—musicians, chess players, athletes, academics—confirm that a willingness to practice is the single most important predictor of success.

Too much ability can even get in the artist's way. During her many years of working with authors, editor-agent Betsy Lerner found that talent not only didn't make writing easier but could even make it harder. Some of the best writers she worked with were some of the most self-sabotaging. "Lack of discipline, desire for fame, and depression often thwart those whose talents appear most fertile," Lerner explained, "while those who struggle with every line persevere regardless." A willingness to submit their work fifty times if necessary, she thought, or revise it repeatedly, distinguished the sung from the unsung more than any contrast in talent.

Unusually talented writers can be like the most graceful

dancer in ballet class whose stage fright keeps her in the wings, or the brilliant blacktop basketball player who never develops the work ethic needed to join less gifted colleagues in the National Basketball Association. It's commonplace for professional athletes to mention better players than they who never left the playgrounds of their youth. The same thing is true of writers. Jack Kerouac, Allen Ginsberg, and others touted Neal Cassady as the most talented writer of them all, making excuses for the fact that he couldn't produce. They could. And it's their names that we know today.

Martha Grimes is another. Grimes's first novel was rejected by dozens of publishers before Little, Brown accepted it and printed 3,000 copies. No matter. Her fifteen subsequent books won Grimes an enormous following. Some were bestsellers. None of this would have been possible if Grimes hadn't kept submitting and resubmitting her first manuscript—"without any encouragement"—until it finally got published.

If you keep writing when every fiber of your being cries "Stop!" you may be a writer. The question at those times is not "Should I stop?" It's "Do I have what it takes?" John Gardner thought the essential ingredient for any novelist was *drivenness*. Theodore Solotaroff talked of *durability*. These are two sides of the same coin. In his excellent essay "Writing in the Cold," Solotaroff noted how many of the most natural writers, "the ones who seemed to shake their prose and poetry out of their sleeves," disappeared after a few early successes. The reason, he thought, was that they lacked the mettle to endure uncertainty, rejection, and disappointment. "The gifted young writer has to learn that his main task is to persist," concluded Solotaroff.

A writer can get by with a modest amount of talent. But none can succeed without stick-to-it-iveness. "If they really stick at it," veteran editor Edward Chase once observed of those who are determined to publish, "eventually—like salmon swimming upstream—they're going to make it." That kind of determination is rare, however, more rare than native ability.

Occasionally one comes across a writer who combines talent with drive. The two in tandem can produce great art. But that is extraordinary. In the meantime, publishers have lists to fill, and they know that they're more likely to fill them from the output of the tenacious than of the talented. If you must choose, therefore, choose tenacity. Tenacity can not only help you get published but is your best ally when dealing with despair. "Fanaticism and dedication and doggedness and stubbornness are your angels," said Charles Baxter. "They keep the demon of discouragement at bay."

3) I Hardly Ever Get Inspired

Somerset Maugham was once asked if he ever got a sudden inspiration for a play. Maugham said he didn't. He never got ideas that way. "I just write for several hours a day at the same time every day," said the playwright and novelist. "Sometimes I just write my name until an idea occurs."

Like talent, "inspiration" is overrated when it comes to writing. The muse is a tease. She is like a charismatic friend with whom it's fun to party—*if* she shows up. Too many writers turn off their computer and turn on the television because they think Ms. Muse has stood them up. It's thrilling to write when inspired, just as making love is most exciting during a torrid romance. But writing careers can no more be based on lightning bolts of inspiration than lasting marriages can be built on hot nights of lusty lovemaking. Serious writers *write*, inspired or not.

Over time they discover that routine is a better friend to them than inspiration. The simple fact of sitting down to write day after day is what makes writers productive. Far from being

unusually inspired, most are remarkably diligent. They are mil-
ers, not sprinters. Few authors consider literary lightning bolts
an essential part of what they do. "I don't know anything about
inspiration because I don't know what inspiration is," said
Faulkner. "I've heard about it, but I never saw it." Novelist
William Kennedy said that while awaiting the muse on his days
off from the *Albany Times-Union*, he usually discovered she
was off that day too.

This isn't to say that working writers never get inspired or
don't bask in inspiration's glow when they do. But they don't
wait for the muse to show up. And when she does, they are
concerned she'll be more harmful than helpful; a trollop
beneath a streetlight, distracting them with her come-hither
look. That is why so many authors scrutinize "inspired" writing
with the greatest suspicion. Frank Yerby actually stopped working when he felt inspired, because he knew he'd have to throw
that writing away. Yerby thought writing a novel was like building a wall, brick by brick. "Only amateurs believe in inspiration," he said.

Like Yerby, many writers use remarkably prosaic analogies
to depict what they do. Anatole France compared writing to
fine carpentry. Both involved planing, France explained, of
wood and sentences. Larry Brown concurred, calling the
apprentice years of any writer little different from those of a
carpenter or bricklayer. Brown thought that writing a book was
like building a house. Doris Lessing accorded her profession a
bit more status than that. Lessing compared writing prose to
the problem solving engaged in by a scientist or engineer. But
muse waiting wasn't part of her equation, either. "I've always
disliked words like *inspiration*," said Lessing.

If the muse does pay a writer a visit, it's most likely to be
early in a project when all is possibility and rewriting has yet
to rear its ominous head. Revision is like the last mile of a

marathon: the exhausting, demanding work necessary to reach the finish line, magnified by an anxious awareness of how close one is to the moment of judgment. Many writers are not up to this challenge. They slump under the weight of their rewritten words. ("*If I have to look at that manuscript one more time . . .* ") One response is to do a cursory job of rewriting. I've read the results too many times, even in published books. Such books read like second drafts, because they usually are (sometimes even first drafts). They are a soufflé pulled from the oven halfway through the baking by an impatient chef. Their prose is labored, wordy, hard to follow. Run-on sentences dart about. Vague language weighs down the page. Clichés prop up muddled thoughts. The text is flaccid, not tight. Repetitions abound. In other words, they read like any early draft. The authors of such books lacked the resolve to heed John Fowles's admonition: "The best cutting is done when one is sick of writing."

This could be seen as a discouraging thought. *Revision! Ugh. I thought writing was all about rocket bursts of creativity.* An alternative interpretation is this: One's ability to rewrite is the key to becoming a writer, far more important than native talent or inspired writing sessions. This ability is based on a capacity to sit tight and do the unglamorous work of cutting and crafting. Recall George Garrett's observation that a willingness to stay with the hard work of revision leveled the playing field among writers of varying gifts. More than anything else, the capacity to rewrite is what distinguishes productive writers from unproductive ones.

Good writers think nothing of revising a manuscript dozens of times, if necessary. Frank O'Connor routinely revised his short stories fifty times or more. Hemingway said he rewrote the ending to *Farewell to Arms* thirty-nine times. (This led S. J. Perelman to report that *he* revised *his* stories thirty-seven times.

"I once tried doing 33," the humorist added, "but something was lacking, a certain—how shall I say?—*je ne sais quoi*.") Donald Hall said he routinely rewrote poems dozens of times and in one case put a piece of verse through 500 revisions!

Many writers only discover what they really want to say while revising their words. How do I know what's really on my mind, they ask, until I write something down, reread, and rewrite it until my thoughts become clear to myself? That process owes next to nothing to inspiration. This is why so many prominent writers say that their gift is more for rewriting than writing. Gore Vidal, who once called himself "an obsessive rewriter," added, "In a way, I have nothing to say, but a great deal to add."

This workaday approach is far more the norm than the exception among professional writers. Is that a discouraging thought? It could be just the opposite. Fie on talent! Bah for inspiration! Don't wait for the muse. *Show up.* This is novelist Rosellen Brown's counsel. Brown called the simple acting of *showing up* with pen in hand or fingers on keys "the first, and possibly the most important, thing that separates the real writer from that glibly smiling face one encounters endlessly at parties who says, 'One of these days when I get some spare time I'm going to write that book.' "

4) I Didn't Study Writing

Sandra West Prowell spent years talking herself out of writing at all. Why? Because the Montana novelist not only had no degree in writing, she had no degree of any kind—not even a high school diploma. "In my mind's eye," Prowell said, "only the educated, degreed academics and journalists had the tools to do what I so badly wanted to do. . . . I cringed when anyone asked me what my educational background was. What if I revealed all and they found out I had no right to have my name on a novel or a review in the *New York Times*?" What got Prowell off the literary dime was earning a GED degree when her children were teenagers. As with *The Wizard of Oz*'s scarecrow, this diploma helped Prowell feel qualified to pursue her dream. Doing so led to positive reviews in the *New York Times* and six-figure advances for her mysteries.

Like the early Prowell, many prospective writers feel inhibited by their skimpy academic credentials. They wonder how someone who never pursued a degree in writing can compete with those who have. Or perhaps they did study writing but didn't do so well. The dyslexic Fannie Flagg spent decades acting rather than writing because she got such bad grades in her college writing classes. Had Flagg only known that a study of professional writers found no correlation whatever between educational background and publishing success (in terms of income), she might have started sooner. The Columbia University sociologists who conducted this study couldn't even find any contrast between writers who had graduated from college and those who hadn't.

Bear in mind that Charles Dickens, Mark Twain, Abraham Lincoln, Dashiell Hammett, H. L. Mencken, George Bernard Shaw, Louis L'Amour, Truman Capote, and William Faulkner had no degrees of any kind. Ernest Hemingway graduated from high school but never went to college. Alice Munro dropped out of Western Ontario University after her sophomore year to get married, William Thackeray left Cambridge in the middle of his second year to take up gambling, F. Scott Fitzgerald fled Princeton one step ahead of flunking out as a junior, and James Fenimore Cooper was expelled from Yale. None took part in a writing program.

As I'll consider more fully in chapter 9, taking courses in writing can have great value: to learn technique, find mentors, and meet peers. The benefits of enrolling in a writing program are less clear. A college classmate of my son's once asked me if I thought getting a Master of Fine Arts (MFA) would help her become a better writer. My response was mixed. Such a program could improve her ability to craft an elegant sentence, I said. If she wanted to teach writing, an MFA was an essential union card. If she aspired to write for the *Sewanee Review* or the *New Yorker*, a graduate writing program would be a good place to learn the literary ropes. Her classmates might later turn up in helpful positions: as editors, reviewers, and the like. She would come in contact with agents, editors, and other useful parties. At the very least, she would be in a setting where writing, and the desire to write, are taken seriously. Out-and-out discouragers are rare in writing programs.

On the other hand, a degree in writing not only wouldn't help her write better but in some ways could even hurt her ability to communicate with readers. As many graduates of writing programs discover to their dismay, the ability to sit down and record words that readers will want to read has little to do with the degree they earned.

Scott Turow studied creative writing at Amherst, then spent four years studying and teaching in Stanford's prestigious writing program. The bestselling, critically acclaimed novelist later observed that he owed little of his success to what he learned at Stanford and a lot to the simple fact that he kept writing in the face of profound frustration and multiple rejections of his early work. One reason this work got rejected was that it hewed too closely to the literary mode he'd learned at Stanford. The novel Turow wrote for his master's degree was rejected by over two dozen publishers. This devastating experience led him to spend three years at Harvard Law School and become first a prosecutor, then a defense attorney. In the process he learned an invaluable writing lesson that was slighted at Stanford: the value of a good story well told. Unlike his writing teachers, the lawyers who introduced Turow to his new profession emphasized that juries are engaged and swayed by storytelling. Watching his colleagues at work, Turow was mesmerized by some of the tales they spun in the courtroom. Juries hung on their every word. So did he. As Turow later wrote, "Thus I suddenly saw my answer to the literary conundrum of expressing the unique for a universal audience: Tell them a good story."

This is a common refrain among those who have degrees from writing programs. It wasn't what they learned there, they say, so much as what they learned afterward that stood them in best stead. Many good writers have MFAs. Whether their writing ability is due to, or despite, having that degree is another issue. This raises the much debated question of whether writing can be taught at all. That debate is somewhat beside the point. Techniques can be taught. But good writing transcends technique. As novelist-teacher David Lodge pointed out, writing students can learn many important lessons about technique—point of view, transitions, voice, time shifting—and become writers as a result. "But no course," he added, "can teach you how to produce a text other people will willingly give up their time—and perhaps their money—to read."

In some cases it's just the opposite. Too many writing programs have become part of a self-contained universe with its own frame of reference. The strong sense of community that can be a virtue there can also become ingrown. Participants hang out together, attend each other's readings, and assign each other's books. Unfortunately, as Gore Vidal observed, these books too often lack "voluntary readers." A good story well told may be what most book buyers want, but it's not what most writing programs teach. They tend to focus on *sentences* more than *stories*. When participants describe someone's work as "a good read" or "a real page-turner," they are not being complimentary. That could be why so few of the writers whose books readers most want to buy have respectable academic credentials. Such reader-friendly writers are usually better at telling tales than polishing prose. As one reviewer said of a Robert Ludlum novel, "It's a lousy book. So I stayed up until 3 a.m. to finish it."

The risk one runs in attending a writing program is that of learning to write more for teachers and classmates than for readers. The smiles and nods awarded your work around a seminar table may encourage writing habits that hinder your ability to reach those beyond that table. A creative writing student once told me that what he liked best about his program was the understanding that participants would take each other's work seriously no matter how much it bored them. That sounds laudable, but consider the consequences. By such means writing programs implicitly condone tedious work. Readers don't agree to be bored. Quite the contrary. They simply set aside work that doesn't hold their attention and find something more compelling to do, like watch television or surf the Net.

What concerned novelist Francine Prose about university writing programs like the one in which she taught was that clear, simple, direct observations such as "it was interesting" or "it was boring" were taboo. Although Prose's own major prayer as a writer was that her work wouldn't bore the reader, her colleagues and students alike searched strenuously for euphemisms to avoid using the dreaded *B* word (*boring*) when critiquing each other's work. According to Prose, writing program participants have no permission to share useful information with each other along the lines of, "I was reading your story, and I went to the refrigerator twenty times because that was what I would rather be doing." Yet this is exactly the type of reaction they face from readers should they have the good fortune to get published.

No editor who wants to remain an editor would base a manuscript evaluation on whether the writer has a degree in writing. Nor would any agent. I once asked literary agent Noah Lukeman if MFA students had an edge when it came to writing and publishing. Lukeman said it was hard to answer that question with a simple yes or no. He'd read some awfully bad work by MFA students, including graduates of prestigious programs. On the other hand, Lukeman said he was favorably impressed that they'd made a two- or three-year commitment to study writing. This suggested a level of seriousness that he found attractive. But Lukeman doubted that the time and expense of earning an MFA were essential for a writer. And, he added, just because a program had big-time authors on its faculty didn't mean it offered big-time teaching. Nor did those enrolled in writing programs necessarily have each other's best interests at heart. As the agent put it, "You are surrounded by ten other writing students who are trying to undermine you."

The essential irrelevance of writing degrees may surprise many aspiring writers. It can come as a revelation that publishers seldom even ask about academic credentials. They're selling books, not degrees. Writing is the most equal of all opportunities. Unless your book requires special expertise or appearances on MTV, editors don't care if you're nine or ninety, have three graduate degrees or dropped out of high school, are drop-dead handsome or have saliva dribbling down your three chins. *Just show me the writing.* A compelling *voice* is what they're looking for, and voice has no degree.

5) I'm the Wrong Age

Whenever I hear this one, I'm tempted to ask, "And what would the right age be?"

Any age is a good age to start writing. In recent years first books have been published by seventeen-year-old wunderkind Nick McDonnell and ninety-eight-year-old great-grandmother Jessie Foveaux. "I'm too young," or "I'm too old," or "I'm too anything," just doesn't cut it. That may be a problem for writers, but it's not for publishers.

At her age, Jessie Foveaux would have been hired for very few jobs, but Warner Books was willing to pay the nonagenarian $1 million for *Any Given Day*, a memoir that Foveaux began at eighty in a writing workshop for senior citizens. Putnam didn't hesitate to buy *And Ladies of the Club*, the first novel of Helen Hoover Santmyer, even though she was an eighty-four-year-old nursing home resident at the time. Retired domestic Freddie Mae Baxter got a six-figure advance from Knopf to publish *The Seventh Child*, her collected stories and opinions, when she was seventy-five.

If you want to write, there is no better time than right now. When it comes to age, there is no such thing as missing the writing boat. The roster of writers who began in middle age includes such luminaries as Charles Frazier, Thomas Cahill, Umberto Eco, Anita Brookner, Joseph Conrad, Isak Dinesen, Stendhal, and Miguel de Cervantes (who turned to writing after stints as a soldier, civil servant, tax collector, and prisoner). Jean Auel only began writing in earnest at forty, after raising the five children she'd borne after marrying at eighteen. Tony Hillerman began his Navajo series in his sixties. Laura Ingalls Wilder published her first novel at sixty-five and her best ones in her seventies. Frank McCourt was sixty-six when he published his first book, *Angela's Ashes*. Harriet Doerr won the National Book Award for her first novel, *Stones for Ibarra*, published when she was seventy-three. Norman Maclean's maiden effort, *A River Runs through It*, came out when he was seventy-four. These are just a few of the many writers who first published late in life.

Middle age and older is a great time to start recording words on paper. Now you've got something to write *about*. That's why I'm always pleased when I walk into a writing class and see some gray heads. I'd much rather read the rough output of a retiree with tales to tell than the polished, evasive prose of a young MFA with little experience outside the classroom. Charley Kempthorne, the teacher who led Jessie Foveaux's writing workshop in Manhattan, Kansas, later recalled how riveting he and her classmates found the handful of pages she'd bring to each week's meeting. As the white-haired great-grandmother read from these pages, Kempthorne would muse about the young creative writing students he'd taught a few years earlier who squealed like stuck pigs when he asked them to write three 2,000-word stories in a four-and-a-half-month semester. They considered themselves writers but wrote very little. Foveaux didn't think of herself as a writer but wrote every day, in a Big Chief notebook on her kitchen table.

It's a myth that creative powers decline with age. Recent discoveries about how plastic the brain remains over time are very encouraging for older writers. Let's go further. Research is confirming the use-it-or-lose-it adage, the common hunch that the more we exercise our brain cells, the better they hold up. Apparently, the best defense against senility is giving your brain a regular workout. What better way to do this than by writing?

The advantages of writing when young are more obvious than those of writing when older. If anything, however, writing improves with age. This could be true of creative acts of all kinds. At least that's been the finding of Frank Barron, a psychologist who spent his career studying creativity. According to Barron, creativity often needs time to blossom. For many of us, childlike adventurousness is released from captivity as we get older. A sociologist who studied 143 older artists found that this was why so many thought time had *enhanced* their creative powers. Not the least reason was that their fear of social scrutiny had declined. Charley Kempthorne said what he liked most about his older memoir students was their irreverence, the fact that they felt free to be themselves and not give a damn. "They're not going to worry any more about what the neighbors think," said Kempthorne.

The crippling fear of ridicule is a deadly censor that can keep even gifted writers mute when young. Along with concern about the opinion of others, terror about the prospect of Looking Foolish wanes over time. After writing eighteen books of dignified nonfiction, Peter Drucker published his first novel at seventy-two. Why did he wait so long? "Because the ultimate test of the writer is the novel and I never had the courage to try it," explained the management consultant. "But once I passed seventy, I was no longer terribly worried about making an ass of myself."

Like Drucker, some discover their creative voice along with their courage late in life. This could be why so many authors who began writing when older have said they couldn't have done it sooner. They *had* to wait. Frank McCourt wrote a version of *Angela's Ashes* in his mid-thirties but couldn't make it work for another three decades. "I hadn't found my voice yet," McCourt explained.

"Found my voice" is actually a misnomer. Everyone has a distinct voice. What everyone doesn't have is the confidence to write in that voice. Some take years or decades to develop this confidence. That's why Carol Shields—who didn't start writing seriously until she was in her forties—doubted that she could have done so before then. It wasn't the distractions of raising five children that held her back so much as embarrassment at the very *idea* of considering herself a writer. "I was probably braver at 40 than I was at 22," said the novelist. "I had a kind of faith in what I was writing, and when you're 22 you don't have that. And I was more honest about the themes that were important."

6) *I'm Too Afraid I'll Fail*

Who isn't? Fear of failure is as much a part of the writing process as using active verbs and showing rather than telling. Regardless of how well their work does in the marketplace, how "successful" they appear, how much money they make, how well they're reviewed, or how many awards they win, all writers live with a sense of not having accomplished what they set out to accomplish. "I work continuously within the shadow of failure," said Gail Godwin. "For every novel that makes it to my publisher's desk, there are at least five or six that died on the way."

Failure is the norm for writers. This is not a self-pitying observation (not always, anyway). Rather, when writers talk about the inevitability of failure, it is simply to make the point that they can never reach their lofty goals. Eudora Welty compared writing to juggling in the sense that it's easy to imagine keeping balls in the air but hard to actually do it. In the same sense, a writer's final product is never as good as the one she imagined. Therefore writers invariably "fail."

When I lecture on "The Courage to Write," one line I cite from the book by that title never fails to ignite a ripple of knowing, rueful laughter. That line comes from an Iris Murdoch novel: "Every book is the wreck of a perfect idea." This is a painful secret that writers share. No work they commit to paper is ever as good as the one they set out to produce. Anthony Burgess said that from the first sentence any book is a failure because the book the writer dreamed of writing has now been destroyed. As a result writers begin every project knowing they will fail; fail to write the book they meant to write. "I start a book and I want to make it perfect," said Joan Didion. "Ten pages in, I've already blown it, limited it, made it less, marred it. That's very discouraging. I hate the book at that point. After a while I arrive at an accommodation: well, it's not the ideal, it's not the perfect object I wanted to make, but maybe—if I go ahead and finish it anyway—I can get it right next time. Maybe I can have another chance."

I've never tried to paint and can only imagine the ferocious struggle artists must engage in as they try to transfer their vision to the canvas. Presumably this is a major source of their energy. Certainly, it is for writers. One reason that writers have such reverence for failure is that it keeps them going. Were they ever to "succeed"—write the book they set out to write—would they dare to try writing another?

Writers are like greyhounds chasing a metal rabbit they know they'll never catch. They're forever pursuing a literary horizon: trying to reproduce the book in their head, knowing it can't be done. That's why writers are so disdainful of those who blithely tell them, "One of these days I'm going to write a book myself." Sometimes these fantasy writers go farther and say they've already got one written. You do? one asks. Where? "Up here," they say, tapping their temple. "In my head. Now it's just a matter of writing it down." One student—a bank vice president—taught by author Robert Massello (*Writer Tells All*) cheerfully announced that she'd completed not one but *three* books this way. She just hadn't had time to record them on paper.

Writers get especially vexed when a nonwriter tells them— as many do—"Once I get the time, I'll write a book of my own," as if time was all it took. Two yellowing clippings in my files—ones I like to pull out now and again for a little chuckle of reassurance—illustrate this delusion. In one, Ferdinand Marcos, the then-president of the Philippines, announced that he planned to go into seclusion for three weeks so he could write not one but two books. In the other, actress Cheryl Ladd told a reporter that in addition to acting in plays she planned to appear in films and a Broadway musical, record an album, tour Europe, have a baby, and write a book. "I plan on being busy," said Ladd.

Being a writer involves sustained *writing*. Writers *write*. This seems to surprise those who think they might give it a shot: get inspired, bang out a book, do some signings, get interviewed, appear on talk shows. Those activities, of course, comprise one half of one percent of a writer's life, if that much. The rest is just hard slogging, alone, with little encouragement and dubious prospects of success. Yet the very likelihood of failure reminds writers that they're doing exactly what they ought to be doing.

I once had a student who enjoyed some success publishing pieces of light humor. I pushed her to try new forms, not just rely on what had worked for her in the past. She demurred; she fretted; she tried to change the subject. Why? Finally my student admitted her real fear: that she might fail. "I hope you do," I replied. What better evidence could there be that she was pushing her boundaries?

Success? Failure? In writing, as in life, these two can be hard to tell apart. Nor is it always clear which is to be preferred. Early in his career Herman Melville enjoyed many bestselling "successes" whose titles we barely remember, then published a catastrophic commercial "failure" called *Moby Dick*. Perhaps that was why Melville called failure "the test of greatness."

Among the very best writers, there is almost a cult of failure. In their minds failure proves one has taken a risk. The bigger the failure, the greater the risk. In pursuits of all kinds, apparent success is too often a result of keeping one's aspirations low. The best authors have far more regard for a defeat suffered while overreaching than a so-called victory won with puny goals. "We will be judged on the splendor of our failures," said Faulkner.

Not-writing writers are typically so afraid of failing, of not producing the great work of art or blockbuster bestseller they'd dreamed of producing, that they freeze. Actual writers know that all their dreams are impossible dreams. They consider them like Ponce de León's Fountain of Youth: an unattainable fantasy, but one that might keep them hacking through jungles anyway. Unlike dropouts, working writers come to terms with the fact that they'll probably never write the work they set out to write. They write anyway.

· · ·

The first section of this book has focused on inner obstacles to writing. I hope it helps writers understand and get past these obstacles. Once they do, however, they must confront a whole new set—external ones—that are thrown in their path by those who read and assess their work. These obstacles can be daunting, but perhaps not as daunting as we imagine. By no means are they insurmountable.

{ II }

LOOKING
OUT

Rites of Rejection

Writers often feel . . . that repeated rejections accompanied by reasoned letters mean that in the end there's no hope. This is simply not true.

John Gardner

No rejection is fatal until the writer walks away from the battle leaving dreams and goals behind.

Jeff Herman, literary agent

When others note the number of books and articles I've published, and call me "prolific," I stifle a chuckle. They have no idea how many of my submissions have been rejected—far more than have been accepted. If I could only take them to my basement and show them the file cabinet labeled *Busted Projects*, the one filled with semideveloped ideas for books, essays, and articles that looked better to me than they did to editors.

Like auditioning actors and tongue-tied suitors, writers learn to live with rejection. For most authors most of the time, rebuff is the norm, embrace the exception. Once your submissions have been rejected a few times, it's easy to take the hint and turn to throwing pots or taking photographs. In some cases this is prudent. In others it's premature. Before checking out the price of kilns or Canons, consider how many successful writers spent years enduring repeated rejection of their work.

An Occupational Hazard

Ursula Le Guin sent out her first story when she was eleven. She got her first acceptance at thirty-three. James Dickey endured years of form rejections before he finally saw handwriting on one that said, "Not bad." According to James Lee Burke's agent, 100 editors turned down *Lost Get-Back Boogie* (including multiple editors at the same house) before Louisiana State University Press bought Burke's first novel for a pittance.

It's a rare writer who doesn't have to hack through a jungle of rejection slips before (and after) getting published. Some of history's best-known books were rejected many times before finally being accepted. *The Ginger Man*, by J. P. Donleavy— now considered one of the best 100 novels ever published— was turned down by thirty-six publishers before it found a home. Despite being represented by a top literary agent and being read by prominent editors, John Knowles's *A Separate Peace* was rejected by every major American publisher who saw it. (London's Secker & Warburg eventually published the classic-to-be.) Future bestsellers such as *The Godfather* and *The Exorcist* were turned down repeatedly before finally getting published. Other books that went through multiple rejections before getting published include: *Dune*; *Ironweed*; *Winesburg, Ohio*; *Kon Tiki*; *The Dubliners*; *Look Homeward, Angel*; *Auntie Mame*; *Peyton Place*; *Love Story*; *A Wrinkle in Time*; *Lust for Life*; *The Day of the Jackal*; *Zen and the Art of Motorcycle Maintenance*; *All Things Bright and Beautiful*; and *Field Guide to the Birds*.

The Catcher in the Rye was turned down by the publisher that had originally asked to see it (Harcourt, Brace). After Little, Brown brought out J. D. Salinger's first novel, it went on to sell more than 60 million copies. This was despite the fact that the *New Yorker* declined to excerpt the future classic because the magazine's editors didn't consider it up to their standards. Earlier, they'd rejected the story on which *The Catcher in the Rye* was based. "We feel that we don't know the central character well enough," a *New Yorker* editor told Salinger's agent.

When it comes to rejection, the *New Yorker* is in a league of its own. Among other things, its editors are renowned for their dispatch in doing so. During years of unsuccessful submissions to that magazine, Cynthia Ozick got so accustomed to having them returned in a week's time that she wrote the editors a cheeky note of pique when they took longer to return one of her pieces. Alice Munro's early stories came back from the *New Yorker* so fast that she had the feeling someone's job there was to send them back. James Thurber felt the same way. Both writers wondered if there was some kind of rejection assembly line at work at the *New Yorker*. After joining that magazine's staff, Thurber discovered that this suspicion wasn't too far off. For years, the *New Yorker* employed an editor named John Chapin Mosher whose job was to read, and usually return, submissions by unpublished writers. "I must get back to the office and reject," Mosher would tell Thurber, toward the end of their many lunches together.

About Town, Ben Yagoda's definitive history of the *New Yorker*, is worth reading for its honor roll of rejected writers alone. According to Yagoda, the carbon copies of decades of *New Yorker* rejection letters that he examined would make "a grim anthology." Or a reassuring one, depending on your perspective. They depict repeated rejection of submissions from the likes of Flannery O'Connor, John Cheever, Raymond Carver, Thomas Pynchon, Joseph Heller, Kurt Vonnegut, Jr., and, in Yagoda's words, "just about every other American writer practicing in the final two-thirds of the twentieth century." Ann Beattie had well over a dozen stories returned by the *New Yorker* before she became its quintessential fiction writer. Raymond Carver's work was rejected so routinely that he stopped sending stories to the *New Yorker* until a new editor specifically asked him to try again.

After he sold a single story to the *New Yorker* in 1941, J. D. Salinger's repeated submissions were turned down until 1947, when the magazine bought "A Fine Day for Bananafish." It then rejected a few more of Salinger's stories (including the one that blossomed into *The Catcher in the Rye*). Yagoda thought this extended hiatus, during which Salinger combined rejection by the *New Yorker* with publication in less prominent magazines, taught the young writer how to channel his talent. Eventually, Salinger dedicated a collection of short stories to Gus Lobrano, the *New Yorker* editor who had done much of the rejecting.

As Salinger came to understand, rebuffs from publishers are part of the writing process. Obviously, too many for too long can blow furiously on the flickering flame of hope. An excess can extinguish its glow altogether. But if we're to write, and keep writing in the midst of adversity, we must come to terms with rejection. Those who have a shot at a writing career become more determined than discouraged by being rebuffed. They bounce back, accept criticism, and grow in response to critiques. The ones who probably won't make it blow off suggestions to improve their work, plead for mercy, blame others, fold up their tents after a few rejections, and retreat to a corner to suck their thumbs and whimper about how misunderstood they are. Not that we don't all suck our thumbs and whimper after having our work rejected. But working writers make it a point to return to their keyboards before their thumbs get too slippery to hit the space bar.

Consider the *Chicken Soup* series. Twenty major publishers thought *Chicken Soup for the Soul* had no commercial prospects. This was despite the fact that its coauthors—Jack Canfield and

Mark Victor Hansen—were experienced speakers and aggressive marketers. According to their agent, Jeff Herman, the subsequent success of the first *Chicken Soup* book and its many spin-offs was due to the fact that its authors would not take no for an answer: "They instinctively understood," said Herman, "that all those rejections were simply an uncomfortable part of a process that would eventually get them where they wanted to be."

To working writers, rejection is like stings to a beekeeper: a painful but necessary part of their vocation. They understand that the return of their work isn't meant as a personal rebuff (or seldom is, anyway). It just feels that way. If we put our*selves* into our written words, as we should, it's hard not to take the rejection of those words as a slap in the face from someone whom we've just tried to kiss. The fear of confronting such pain, or the inability to do so more than a few times, makes even promising writers spend more time in front of a television screen than a computer monitor.

At the age of forty-eight, F. X. Toole gave up writing and took up boxing because he could no longer stand the pain— of rejection. Even after multiple injuries in the ring, Toole still considered the agony of a right cross or left jab less excruciating than having his writing returned by an editor. Getting rejected, he told Terry Gross, hurt far more than having his nose flattened. "No comparison," said Toole. "I'd take a broken nose any old day."

There's more to the story, however. At the age of seventy, twenty-two years after throwing in his literary towel, F. X. Toole got back in the writing ring and published *Rope Burns*, a collection of his stories, and one novella.

Rejection, to writers, is the equivalent of being knocked down as a boxer, being heckled as a comedian, or not getting callbacks as an auditioning actor: something they must learn to

endure. One test of a writer is his or her ability to keep rejections in perspective, even to make use of them. Theodore Solotaroff felt that how a writer dealt with rejection was the key to
whether he or she had a literary vocation or merely a flair. "To
put the matter as directly as I can," the editor wrote, "rejection
and uncertainty and disappointment are as much a part of a
writer's life as snow and cold are of an Eskimo's: they are con-
ditions one has to learn not only to live with but also to make
use of."

Recycling Rejection

Throughout his undergraduate years in college, every one of
the many magazines to which Andre Dubus submitted his short
stories sent them back. After a story of his was returned by
Atlantic Monthly, Dubus wrote at the bottom of an *Atlantic*
subscription pitch, "When you buy from me, I'll buy from
you." Dubus then attached this to yet another story and sent
it to the *Atlantic*. That didn't produce a sale but did make the
young writer feel better. Dubus called this process "volunteering
for rejection." It was something he engaged in willingly, beginning at nineteen, to toughen himself. Dubus's strategy worked.
"I have never," he later wrote, "since then, been deeply hurt or
disappointed by the rejection of a story."

Most aspiring writers collect bushels of rejection slips.
Rather than give these pieces of paper the power to lay them
low, as F. X. Toole did, some take the Dubus approach and
de-fang them. In the process a few show remarkable inventive-
ness. They make a purse from the sow's ear of rebuff. As a
young advertising man, F. Scott Fitzgerald pinned the 122 rejection slips he had accumulated in a frieze on the walls of his
room. Muriel Rukeyser made wastebaskets out of her letters of
rejection. Early in his career, when turndowns far outnumbered

acceptances, Stephen King put rejection notes on his dartboard. During downcast days he would lift his spirits by throwing darts at them. ("There, that's it for you, *Cosmopolitan*. There, that's it for you, *McCall's*. Take that, *Alfred Hitchcock*!")

After e. e. cummings's mother paid to have her son's book *No Thanks* published, the poet designed this anti-dedication page:

NO
THANKS
TO

Farrar & Rinehart
Simon & Schuster
Coward-McCann
Limited Editions
Harcourt, Brace
Random House
Equinox Press
Smith & Haas
Viking Press
Knopf
Dutton
Harper's
Scribner's
Covici-Friede

Sharp-eyed readers noted that this list of the fourteen publishers who had rejected *No Thanks* was arranged in the shape of a funeral urn.

The most creative approach of all is to use rejections as writing fodder. Long before he won the Nobel Prize for literature in 2002, Imre Kertesz spent a decade trying to get his first novel (*Fateless*) published. The experience stood him in good stead, however. Kertesz based his second novel (*Fiasco*) on the frustration of a writer who spends years trying to get his first novel published. Similarly, "The Pension Grillparzer"—John Irving's story-within-a-story in his novel *The World according to Garp*—had actually been rejected as "only mildly interesting" by the *Paris Review*, an episode Irving made part of his novel.

Rejection Hubris

All of this is a roundabout way of making one simple point: rejection is a writer's rite of passage. There is even a kind of rejection hubris among some writers. ("You think *you* got rejected by a lot of publishers? Well, let me tell you how many times *I've* been rejected.") Some Web sites post letters of rejection, hoping to numb the pain of contributors by spreading it around. Think of them as an electronic Rejected Anonymous. The Web site of Dan Gutman, an author of children's books, features a Read My Rejection page which includes rejection letters for his novel *Honus & Me*, in part to rub that book's success in the nose of editors who turned it down.

As we've seen, some of our greatest authors experienced repeated rejection before their writing was finally published. Not that publication stanched the bleeding. Rejection is part of the writing life, pre- *and* postpublication. Well into successful careers, even writing luminaries have submissions returned. Isaac Bashevis Singer and Saul Bellow both had work turned down by magazines after they won the Nobel Prize for literature. Singer even saw some value in having post-Nobel work rejected because it proved that this work was being judged on its quality, not just on the fact that his name on the cover might help sell a magazine. At the very least, putting his work on the table for a thumbs-up or thumbs-down reassured the octogenarian that he was still active, still in the game. The only way to stop getting rejected, Singer thought, was to stop writing.

After having his post-Nobel story "Cousins" returned by the *New Yorker*, Saul Bellow too thought this wasn't altogether a bad thing. The turndown forced Bellow, like any rebuffed writer, to rely on his own judgment and say, "To hell with you" to those who returned his work.

Why Did They Have to Publish My Book?

Bellow wasn't always so philosophical about being rejected. Early on, he found the return of his work excruciating. After having his first submission to the *New Yorker* sent back, Bellow took to sending his stories to a sympathetic editor there in the guise of asking for feedback on a work in progress. This editor, in turn, would only show Editor in Chief William Shawn the work by Bellow that she thought had a chance of being bought. When letting the author know that they'd like to publish one of these stories, Bellow's editor would explain that she "hadn't been able to resist showing it to Mr. Shawn." This subterfuge worked perfectly for everyone involved.

In hindsight, Bellow was grateful that much of his fledgling work did not get accepted. An early novel by him would have been published had World War II not intervened. On reflection and rereading, Bellow was so relieved it wasn't that he threw the manuscript down an incinerator chute. Not all writers are so fortunate. Those "luckier" than Bellow, who get raw early work published, often spend their later years chasing down copies of these books so they can destroy them. "I think being rejected can be very beneficial," said Stephen King, whose first four novels and sixty stories were returned to sender, "especially if the work isn't good. If it gets published, you are almost certain to find yourself looking back with great embarrassment!"

On a train, Hilaire Belloc saw the passenger seated in front of him reading his *History of England*. Belloc asked the man how much he had paid for the book. When told the figure, Belloc took that amount from his wallet, put it in the man's left hand, grabbed *History of England* from the right one, and threw it out the train car's window.

In the Mortification Hall of Fame, there is a special wing for the early works of noted authors. Robert Graves continually revised his own published collections, deleting poems that he thought had been written for the wrong reasons, ones that gave him "a sick feeling." Marianne Moore would only sign books after first making corrections in copies thrust at her by book buyers.

Based on such accounts, fledgling writers who are having trouble getting their work in print might want to consider the alternative: premature publication. In some cases the only thing worse than having too much work rejected is not having enough come back. One of the biggest obstacles I had to overcome early in my own career was publishing an article in a major national magazine for the then-princely sum of $2,000. It was quite some time before I enjoyed a comparable payday. Eventually, I had to return to writing for smaller outlets and learn my craft better. In the long run this was the best thing that could have happened to me.

Hilma Wolitzer had a similar experience. In 1965 the aspiring novelist sold a short story to a national magazine for $1,250. Wolitzer used the money to buy herself a new car, confident that this was just the first of many big paychecks to come. It was three years before she sold another story, to a small literary magazine, for a pittance. That was when Wolitzer turned to teaching, adult education classes first, then the likes of Iowa Writers' Workshop and Breadloaf students.

One of her students at Iowa was Michael Cunningham. Cunningham was a promising young writer who sold stories to *Atlantic Monthly* and *Paris Review* while still being taught by Wolitzer.

This led him to conclude that writing and publishing weren't as hard as he'd imagined. For years Cunningham sent stories he considered as good as the ones he'd published to the magazines that had accepted them, only to get these stories back, virtually by return mail. He wondered if they were even being read. Finally, Cunningham published a novel (*Golden States*) that got good reviews and few readers. For the next several years, as Cunningham tended bar and waited on tables, *New Yorker* editor Daniel Menaker rejected so many of his stories that—like Alice Munro and James Thurber before him—Cunningham began to wonder if this was Menaker's only job. Finally, however, Menaker helped him get a promising story polished enough to publish. This story received so much favorable attention that Cunningham's agent heard from book editors who wanted to see a novel by the now-not-so-young author. Michael Cunningham has since enjoyed the kind of critical and commercial success—including a Pulitzer Prize for *The Hours*—that he was sure would be his nearly two decades earlier.

One could argue that a writer such as Cunningham might have been better served by less success early on, and a bit more aggravation. Early obstacles have their value. The worst thing that could happen to an aspiring writer would be to have too much early work accepted in its original form. Those for whom writing and publication come easily don't find it necessary to develop the grit and drive they'll need to stay the course. They get too little practice at coping with frustration. Novelist Stephen Cannell said his greatest asset as a writer was the severe dyslexia that forced him to develop his powers of imagination and learn how to push ahead in the face of disappointment. The fact that he was dyslexic also meant that little was expected from Cannell in school. "It never occurred to me to try to be perfect," he said, "so I've always been happy as a writer just to entertain myself."

The literary record is littered with one-book wonders such as Ralph Ellison, Henry Roth, Hannah Green, Malcolm Lowry, Margaret Mitchell, and Harper Lee, whose writing hand froze after a single early triumph. Early acclaim makes it that much harder to develop the skill, range, and tenacity to be a writer of books rather than the author of a book.

Texas author Billie Lee Brammer enjoyed great success with a first novel called *The Gay Place*. When his friend Larry King called to read Brammer the lavish praise his book had received in the *New York Times Book Review*, the Texan's response was, "Oh, Jesus, now they'll be waiting to pin my ears back if I can't do it again." Brammer never did, and a few years later died of a drug overdose. "Had Brammer received a few critical pokes and a stomping or two, as usually happens with first novelists," King wrote, "—except when they are ignored— might he then have been motivated to prove the bastards wrong and keep on working?"

Early flashes tend to get panned later, sometimes by the very critics who initially praised them. Authors of acclaimed first books have huge bull's-eyes hung around their necks on second ones. This could be why so few first novelists ever publish a second time. Writers who learn their craft more slowly, steadily, building their resolve like a novice prizefighter, learn to endure rejection, keep it in perspective. They develop the carapace to protect themselves from slings and arrows in the course of a long-term career. If one's writing has been rejected a lot, said Madeleine L'Engle—as hers was—"success is extra pleasant, but not to be taken too seriously."

The Vagaries of Rejection

Rejection is based on two variables: the inherent quality of a writer's work, and an editor's assessment of that quality. It's dangerous and self-indulgent to assume that the return of our submissions only reflects poor editorial judgment. ("They just don't *get* it.") But it can be equally dangerous to assume out of hand that rejection is an accurate evaluation of our writing. Doing this compounds outer rejection with the inner kind. ("What ever made me think I could write, anyway?") We put ourselves in the docket and plead guilty to an editor's verdict. Memo to Self: *Stop writing!* That could be sound advice. More likely it's precipitate. As we'll see in the next two chapters, work gets returned for all kinds of reasons. One is that a piece of writing is not very good, or at least not very publishable. Other reasons include: wrong publisher for the work in question; publisher has a similar book under contract; or the editor involved is about to change jobs, having a bad hair day, or just doesn't care for your kind of project.

James Thurber once intercepted a story by Astrid Peters that *New Yorker* editor John Mosher had rejected because it dealt with a woman's adolescence, a topic Mosher considered "tedious." Thurber persuaded the *New Yorker*'s head editor, Harold Ross, to buy it anyway. This story was subsequently reprinted in *The Best American Short Stories* for that year.

Ann Beattie's collection *Distortions* includes many stories rejected by the *New Yorker*. Lorrie Moore's *Self-Help* consists primarily of stories returned to her by magazine editors. The idea for Rachel Carson's classic book *Silent Spring* had been turned down as a possible article by the *Reader's Digest*. The story on navigation that Dava Sobel couldn't sell to a mainstream magazine later enjoyed great success as a book called *Longitude*.

Manuscripts are returned to sender for an infinite number of reasons, many of which have little to do with their quality or even the validity of an editor's judgment. In some cases it can simply be a matter of bad timing. After the collapse of the World Trade Center in 2001, editors at the *New Yorker* found themselves returning short stories they might have accepted just a few days earlier. The national mood had changed that much. The *New Yorker*'s fiction editor said one colleague attached to a submission a note that read, "I liked this story, but that was before September 11. Now it doesn't seem right."

Experiences such as these teach experienced writers not to put too much weight on rejections. Some are downright laughable, especially in hindsight.

- *The Diary of Anne Frank* was returned by one publisher who wrote, "The girl doesn't, it seems to me, have a special perception or feeling, which would lift that book above the 'curiosity' level."
- Paul Bowles's classic, *The Sheltering Sky*, was rejected by Doubleday—the publisher that had contracted for it—as "not a novel."
- One editor called John Knowles's *A Separate Peace* "embarrassingly overwrought" and concluded, "I feel rather hopeless about his having a future."
- Based on his reading of *The Last of the Plainsmen*, a Harper's editor told Zane Grey, "I don't see anything in this to convince me you can write either narrative or fiction." (After accepting a subsequent novel by Grey, the same editor said, "You've done it. You've made me eat my words.")

Frank O'Connor thought an amusing anthology could be created from rejection letters. (Since he said that, one has appeared, *Rotten Rejections*, from which some of the preceding gaffes are excerpted.) O'Connor himself once had a story accepted by a *New Yorker* editor. After touching up the story, he returned it to the magazine. This version landed on the desk of a different editor. That editor wrote the novelist a polite letter saying that although they couldn't use his story, they would like to see future work by him.

I had a similar experience. The articles editor of *Good House-keeping* gave me an assignment to write an essay for this magazine. A few weeks later I sent her the completed manuscript. Two weeks after that it came back with a form rejection slip attached. The piece had never reached its intended destination and had been rejected by a first reader. (The embarrassed articles editor asked me to return my essay and eventually published it.)

In the annals of publishing, no rejections stand out more vividly than those endured by George Orwell for his novel *Animal Farm.* In a cool rejection letter, Faber editor T. S. Eliot told Orwell that although the satiric fable had certain virtues, "I regret to say that it does not appear to me possible as a publishing venture." Eliot was not alone in his assessment. After *Animal Farm* was turned down by three more English editors, Orwell made preparations to publish it himself. Before he could do so, however, the novel was accepted by Secker & Warburg, which had earlier published Orwell's much-rejected *Homage to Catalonia.* The phenomenal success of *Animal Farm* and its follow-up, *1984,* put Secker & Warburg on the map. "*Animal Farm* made me as a publisher," said Frederic Warburg.

Why was Orwell's book so problematic for other publishers? One reason was that it wasn't easy to categorize. Was it a novel or a novella? A fable or a political tract? And was it meant for kids, adults, or both? In publishing argot, *Animal Farm* "fell between two stools." This seemed to be a particular problem for American publishers. A dozen of them passed on *Animal Farm,* including Harper's, Knopf, Viking, Dial, and Scribner. Harper's first reader thought the book's fantasy was unconvincing and its audience unclear. The reader recommended turning it down. Harper's publisher later said that accepting this recommendation without reviewing the manuscript himself was one of his all-time biggest blunders. He had plenty of company. At Dial, an editor rejected Orwell's manuscript with the explanation that stories about animals were impossible to sell in the United States. When the English edition showed some life, another Dial editor wrote Orwell saying there had been some mistake in its first reading there and could Dial have another look. By that time Harcourt, Brace had bought *Animal Farm*'s North American rights. Even then Harcourt's publisher fretted that readers might miss Orwell's satiric point. When the Book-of-the-Month Club selected the novel, however, his nerves were soothed. The Book-of-the-Month Club alone sold 500,000 copies of *Animal Farm*. Orwell's masterpiece went on to be purchased by millions of book buyers around the world.

In and of themselves, such stories are encouraging. Publishers do make mistakes, possibly even the ones who don't buy our work. But it's important to understand the context—why these errors of judgment recur year after year, decade after decade, century after century. As we'll see in the next two chapters, there are a wide variety of reasons for rejecting writers' work that have as much to do with the culture of publishing as the quality of the work. My hope is that these chapters will help writer-readers feel less in awe of a world that can seem so intimidating. Their intent is not so much to debunk as to demystify the world of publishing. To accomplish this goal, an anthropological perspective is far more useful than a literary one.

· 6 ·

The Publishing Tribe

Publishing is a very mysterious business.

Thomas Wolfe

A wise publisher's sales representative once advised me to learn enough about publishing to deal knowledgeably with its members, but not so much that I'd get completely discouraged and decide to raise llamas rather than write books. Any prospective writer could benefit from that advice. Becoming reasonably familiar with the ways of publishers, editors, agents, subsidiary rights directors, publicists, marketing directors, advertising managers, sales reps, and booksellers—those I call *pub people*—is to a writer's advantage. We wouldn't visit Papua New Guinea without reading a bit about its local customs. Nor should we approach the world of publishing without first learning something of its ways.

What follows is one writer's take on that world. It is based on elements familiar to those who work there, and some writers of long standing, but rarely to those first approaching the Oz of major trade publishing. The fact that so many pub people work in the great and wondrous city of New York makes them that much more intimidating to writers who don't. Even Pat Conroy—who writes with such searing candor about himself and his family—pleaded with the editor of one of his novels: "Anything that would cause people to laugh at me, or tease me in New York City, please get rid of it."

One novelist told me that before meeting some, she imagined that every woman who worked in publishing wore pinstriped business suits and six-inch stiletto heels, had nails polished Chinese red, and eyebrows shaped to a forbidding arch. In fact, they're more likely to resemble Nicole Kidman's Virginia Woolf than Joan Crawford's dragon lady. In general pub people are like Oz's Wizard: anxious folks throwing up lots of smoke, trying to appear more omniscient than they really are. About like the rest of us. The intent of this chapter is to reduce your anxiety when dealing with pub people by making them more human, more comprehensible, and by emphasizing your value to them.

Keep in mind: *They need you more than you need them.* Writers don't *need* agents, editors, publicists, or sales reps. (As I'll discuss in chapter 10, some publishing visionaries foresee a digitized future in which authors bypass such middlemen and reach readers directly.) All writers need is paper and pen, or computer and keyboard. Agents, on the other hand, need writers to represent, editors need their manuscripts to edit, publicists their books to publicize, and sales reps must have them to sell. Without writers the whole enterprise would collapse. Writers are the linchpin of publishing. You are a very valuable commodity. Act like it. Not cocky, arrogant, or bristling with attitude. Just cognizant of your own value. As it is, too many writers are too prone to engage in *submission*, in every sense of the word.

The imperious manner of some pub people encourages this proneness. No matter how likely it may seem, however, agents and editors are not singling you out for special disdain. In fact—don't take this personally—you are not uppermost in their minds. Those who publish books have too many other things to think about: themselves, each other, and, of necessity, booksellers. (An editor told author Robert Massello that he and his colleagues had "flings" with those who write books but were married to those who sell them.) What they *do* have on their mind are things you ought to know about. The best way to educate yourself about publishing is to put this world in a context that makes sense. Nervous speakers are advised to imagine their listeners naked. Anxious writers might want to envision pub people as their high school classmates.

Why Publishing Resembles High School

After spending three years writing *The Blessing Way*, Albuquerque's Tony Hillerman sent this novel to his agent in New York. The agent sent it back. Why? Because she wouldn't dare risk her reputation by showing his manuscript to editors there whom she knew would be put off by Hillerman's depiction of Navajo ways. "If you insist on rewriting this," the author said she told him, "get rid of all that Indian stuff." Instead, he got rid of her. Hillerman's Navajo-based novels went on to become one of the most successful mystery series of all time.

Why didn't his agent recognize their potential? Because she was a product of her social milieu. We all are. We're all mindful of the attitudes of those with whom we see regularly. It's hard not to be more influenced by the norms of peers we see often (e.g., other pub people) than those of ones we see seldom (such as writers and readers). Call it *peer fear*. Anxiety about our peers' opinion and a fine appreciation of their tastes make it difficult to consider anything that might deviate from those tastes. When Tony Hillerman sent his agent *The Blessing Way*, the notion of mingling Navajo spirituality with soft-boiled detective fiction seemed absurd. Hillerman might as well have asked her to join him for lunch at the Four Seasons wearing a lime-colored polyester pants suit.

Does this sensibility sound familiar? Perhaps like the one in your high school? If so, that's no coincidence. Teenagers everywhere are a tribal bunch. So are pub people, and on much the same terms. To make the world of publishing come into clearest focus, recall your adolescence: the crowds, cliques, rivalries, jealousies, intrigue, gossip, slang, buzz words, fashions, fads, and who ate lunch where and with whom. That's publishing. "You're wondering if the people at the cool table will snub you," said one editor of his regular lunches at a Manhattan restaurant favored by media types.

The only basic difference between pub people and your high school classmates is that pub people have more money and bigger vocabularies. Like adolescents everywhere, they are far more concerned about the opinion of those they consider part of their crowd than those they don't. I hate to be the one to break this to you, but pub people don't necessarily consider writers to be in with this crowd. Why should they? Writers are loners. They spend so much time by themselves that they lose their social skills, become edgy, kvetchy, antisocial, self-absorbed, self-pitying, self-aggrandizing, insecure, and paranoid. Not good company. In fact, their ways are so different from pub people's ways that they might as well come from a different tribe altogether.

The Writing Way, the Publishing Way

Pub people have their ways. Writers do too. Like many of my colleagues, I find an afternoon nap is indispensable if I'm to accomplish anything after lunch. Naps are a writer's perk. I realize that they have a fishy odor among those with day jobs, so my kids have strict instructions to tell anyone who calls me while I'm asleep, "He can't come to the phone right now." When one of them slipped and told an editor I was napping, that editor later chided me for my indolent ways. "*I* don't get to nap," he said.

True. But, as I reminded him, he did get Xerox privileges, a dental plan, and occasional tickets to Knicks games.

Such contrasts in context can make it hard for publishing people and writers to get on the same page. Of necessity, editors are focused on getting manuscripts in that can be published on the promised date. (As one told me—only semifacetiously— "If it's done, it's good.") It is easy for them to see writers who have trouble keeping that commitment as unreliable, spoiled children. "Stop whining and get a real job," suggested one agent. "The world does not owe you a living you can perform in your pajamas!"

That last one got into sensitive territory. Writers are touchy about their dress code, or lack of one. A few dress up to write; most dress down; some don't dress at all. Does this make them less than grown up? They worry about such things. At the same time they revel in their sartorial freedom and contempt for convention. George Bernard Shaw said the main reason he took up writing was that, "as the author is never seen by his clients, he need not dress respectably."

You begin to see why these two tribes have communication issues. We're dealing with two very different worldviews here. Writers almost never become pub people, and pub people seldom become writers. Their sensibilities are too distinct. Each has their own ways, many of which are at variance with the other's.

PUB PEOPLE	WRITERS
Up early	Up whenever
Nap seldom	Nap often
Dress up	Dress down (if at all)
Work well with others	Work best alone
Office politics	No one to politic
Lunch a lot	Lunch a little
Behind the scenes	On stage

Schedule-driven	Vague sense of time
Could get fired	Already unemployed
Paycheck, benefits	Irregular income, no benefits
Can read a P & L sheet	What's P & L?

Tribal Customs

A publisher's marketing director once suggested calling a book of mine 'Til the Fat Lady Sings. According to my editor, everyone there thought this was a great idea (or at least kept their counsel). All I could think of was the many overweight women who have attended any book signing I've ever done. How was I going to get them excited about my Fat Lady book? Anyone I talked to outside of publishing circles understood this problem immediately. My editor did not, however, nor did my agent, or any other pub person I consulted. In exasperation I asked a slim publisher's consultant in Manhattan if she had any fat friends. "I wouldn't!" the consultant replied. (She was kidding, of course, and yet . . .) Only then did I realize what the problem was: obesity is not that big an issue in publishing. Among all the agents, editors, and sundry publishing types I've known over the years, few were seriously overweight. Many were skin and bones. By contrast with other settings, publishing is a positively anorexic environment.

Pub people are a breed apart. Like any group of people intensely involved with each other over an extended period of time, those who publish books have become a neoindigenous people. They have mores, folkways, legends, taboos, shamans, status display, belief systems, ceremonies, and customs. Their rituals can be puzzling to outsiders: blurbing, jacket conferencing, navigating piles of slush. Ceremonial bread-breaking takes place in various kinds of lunches: deal lunches with agents, political lunches with each other, stroke-the-author lunches in which hungry writers are encouraged to order without regard for the right-hand side of the menu. Then there's the semi-annual sales conference—publishing's *carnaval*—where pub people travel to exotic locales as a reward and escape and an opportunity to blow off steam in ways that might raise eyebrows back at the home office. During the conference itself they discuss which books they hope will *have legs*, which authors are *tourable*, and what books have *slipped*, or had their publication date postponed.

Pub people say that one reason they like to deal with each other is because they "speak the same language." This is literally true. Like any indigenous group, those in publishing have their own vocabulary. Unsolicited manuscripts that come *over the transom* get thrown in *the slush pile*. A thumbnail sketch of a book and its raison d'être are its *sales handle*, or *hook*. The percentage of books that booksellers buy but don't return constitutes the *sell-through* rate. Free shipping is called *freight pass-through*.

Writers—new ones especially—are seldom fluent in pub-speak. It's an unnecessary source of awe, one of many barriers to communication between these two tribes. They're like residents of Paris and Port-au-Prince who speak the same language but with such different dialects that they have frequent failures to communicate. There is no need for writers to become fluent in the nomenclature of publishing. But it would help to have a phrase book.

When you're dealing with pub people, it helps to know the difference between a book's *jacket* and its *cover*, or to distinguish a *footnote* from a *source note* from an *endnote*. *Page proofs* are not the same thing as *galley proofs*, which in turn must be distinguished from *bound galleys*. As their names imply, *front matter* (contents, dedication, preface, acknowledgments) is quite different from *back matter* (source notes, index, etc.). The physical dimensions of a book don't just constitute its size but its *trim size*. A *skip* is a book with so few prospects in the marketplace that sales reps don't even mention it to booksellers. Books that are ordered but don't sell have as short a *shelf life* as a container of yogurt.

Much publishing terminology consists of old words repurposed. To pub people, a *spine* is not just something that aches after too many hours at a desk but the narrow side of a book which is the only part usually seen by bookstore customers (because most are shelved *spine out* in bookstores, not *face out*). *Orphans* are books that were acquired by an editor who then resigns, leaving that book without an in-house parent. A *house* is a publishing company that publishes seasonal *lists* of books (*winter list, spring list, fall list*). *List* is an important concept in publishing because it gets coupled with so many other concepts. Recently published books constitute a publisher's *frontlist*; ones that stay in print long after their *pub date* join the *backlist*. Writers with modest sales records are called *midlist authors*.

To *crash* a book is to publish it quickly, as was done for books about 9/11. An older meaning of the word *crash* was the coarse fabric that reinforced the spine of bound volumes. The term *blurb* was coined in 1907, by an author who thought such puffery could be portrayed best by a made-up word that mimicked sounds made by publishers. *Trade books*, or "books to the trade," are general-interest titles (as opposed to textbooks, reference books, or mass-market paperbacks). This term derives from London booksellers in Dr. Johnson's time being called "the Trade."

Their different dialects are just one among many contrasts between pub people and those whose work they publish. Further magnifying the gulf between these two tribes is the fact that one is headquartered on an island off the coast of New Jersey. This gap is not just a matter of geography but the source of continual misunderstandings between editors who work in New York and writers who don't.

Territoriality

While living in San Diego, I could not interest any New York–based editor in a story about what people do when they're alone in cars. Editors in Los Angeles loved the idea, and two bought articles from me on that subject. On the other hand, I had no trouble at all getting an editor at *New York* magazine interested in an article about what people do when they're alone in elevators, a topic that bored editors in L.A.

When making decisions about what manuscripts to accept, pub people consult their own sensibility first, as they should. That sensibility is highly influenced by their surroundings, however. This is true of us all. Our settings shape our outlooks. It makes no difference whether these settings feature co-ops or condos, Zabar's or Sav-On, Wal-Mart or Wall Street.

This was never more clear to me than the day I floated an idea for a book on *The Secret Life of Malls* with a couple of agents in Manhattan. Shopping malls have always intrigued me. These settings are not as bland as they appear, and I thought readers might be interested in the scheming, conflict, and coupling that goes on behind their placid exteriors. One agent agreed that some readers might buy this book, but not enough to warrant a big sale. She herself, the agent added, had never set foot in a shopping mall. Nor did she ever intend to. The second agent was more adamant. "*That book doesn't sell!*" she replied without hesitating when I brought up my mall idea. Her response itself didn't surprise me as much as its vehemence. It was as if I'd proposed writing a sympathetic study of pedophilia. Whether or not a book on the inner life of shopping malls made commercial sense still isn't clear to me. What is clear is how representative members of New York's publishing community feel about malls.

One source of writers' frustration is the disconnect between the lives of those who don't work in New York and the many editors who do. This is not a knock on their home base. If most writing was done in Manhattan but most publishing in Topeka, the same problem would exist in reverse. I'm inordinately fond of New York and New Yorkers (including the one to whom I'm married). My point is not that this city and those who live there need to be brought down a peg or two. My only point is that for those who are based in such a distinctive setting, generalizing from their own day-to-day experience to that of writers and readers is problematic. Yet pub people do, unwittingly, all the time. When Ann Beattie included the name of her small Connecticut town in a story that the *New Yorker* accepted, Beattie's edited copy included a notation beside the town's name reading, "No such place." Fort Myers author Jonellen Heckler was advised by her Manhattan agent that an episode in her Florida-based novel in which a character forced his way through the front door of an apartment did not ring true. Why? "Because the doorman would have stopped him."

After he sold over a quarter million copies of his self-published book *The Christmas Box*, Utah author Richard Paul Evans had an article turned down by an editor at a major magazine in Manhattan. "You could not possibly have sold that many books," the editor told him. "No one in New York has heard of you." Once publishers confirmed his sales figures and began to clamor for rights to *The Christmas Box*, a book editor asked Evans where exactly Utah was.

"Between New York and L.A.," he replied.

"Well, if you see any other books out there," said this editor, "let us know."

Like island residents everywhere, Manhattan-based pub people have their own frame of reference. Most tend to watch the same shows, talk to people like themselves, attend each other's parties, and read identical publications. (A Boston-based editor told me he only had to pay a modest sum for a comic strip collection that became a very successful book because the strip did not run in any New York newspaper, although it did appear in the *Boston Globe*.) *Publishers Weekly* and publisher-slunch.com routinely include stories about agents and editors who happen on book ideas when reading the *New York Times*, *New York*, and *New York Observer*, or by hearing about them on a Manhattan radio or television station. In other words, they get ideas as we all do—by taking note of what's around them. Only what's around them is high-rises, yellow cabs, delicatessens, and subways, not malls, SUVs, Sam's Club, and Subway.

Nancy Zafris, the fiction editor at the *Kenyon Review*, wrote a novel about metalworkers in her hometown of Columbus, Ohio. This made it a hard sell for some editors at major trade publishers. "Who wants to read about some guy working in Columbus, Ohio?" one asked her. Zafris was savvy enough to realize that if she moved her metalworkers to Manhattan and had two of her characters meet cute while fighting over a lone poppy seed bagel at the Second Avenue Deli, her novel would have more resonance for these editors than if they met over a sack of sliders (small hamburgers steamed with onions) at a White Castle on High Street in Columbus. Fortunately a broad-minded editor at Penguin saw beyond its locale and published Zafris's novel, *The Metal Shredder*, Columbus and all.

The important point here is not just that Zafris had trouble breaking through a mind-set that had trouble envisioning anything of interest happening in a medium-sized midwestern city, but that eventually she did make this breakthrough. There *are* editors who are open to writing that doesn't match up with their tribal perspective. William Thompson, for example, enjoys the distinction of having published first books by both John Grisham and Stephen King after so many of his colleagues had returned their work. King thought that trade editors as a group were at a disadvantage when it came to commercial fiction, however, because they were not familiar with, or sympathetic to, the elements of everyday American iconography—the fast-food outlets, supermarkets, and strip malls—that a writer like him wove into his books, and that struck so many chords of recognition with readers. Those editors were far better at recognizing excellent literary fiction, King believed, than works that might appeal to a broad book-buying public.

Shrewd members of New York's publishing community are painfully aware that most major waves of publishing now gather force beyond the Holland Tunnel. Manhattan-based pub people try desperately to spot and ride those waves, but they're working at a disadvantage. Their vision is obscured both by geographic and cultural isolation. An observation made by Berkeley author-editor Ernest Callenbach three decades ago remains as true as ever: "There are a lot of things going on out here which don't make sense in New York." Callenbach should know. He said the main reason that nearly two dozen New York publishers turned down his futuristic novel *Ecotopia* was because "they thought the ecological 'fad' was over." This was in 1974.

New York–based publishers realize better than anyone how circumscribed they are by borders of place and taste. The smartest among them know that their vision is restricted by tall buildings, but aren't sure what to do about it. They're not necessarily *opposed* to writing that reflects heartland sensibilities; it just doesn't resonate with them. To a surprising degree, pub people base editorial decisions on their own predilections. An editor at a major trade publisher once returned a manuscript to agent Oscar Collier with the explanation that he didn't care for books about California. At least this editor was candid and didn't try to generalize his bias. Certainly, it was the editor's prerogative to not publish a book on a topic that bored him.

All editors have their own tastes. But when too many of these tastes are at variance with those of readers, problems ensue.

Matters of Taste

John Berendt's then-agent—one of New York's most prestigious—chose not to represent his Georgia-based work of nonfiction. According to Berendt, she was put off by the drag queens, eccentrics, and lowlifes he portrayed. His agent also felt the book's Savannah setting was "too local." And wasn't its title rather long? This decision cost Berendt's former agent a small fortune in commissions on his mega-bestseller *Midnight in the Garden of Good and Evil*. And it wasn't his agent alone who saw no promise in Berendt's book. She was simply conveying the collective wisdom of her tribe to the author. According to editor-agent Betsy Lerner, "Almost anyone in the publishing industry would have told him nobody would care about the story of a gay antiques dealer who languished in jail after shooting a cheap hustler."

This is where the rubber hits the road when it comes to editorial decisions. Editors routinely rely on their own taste when deciding what to accept and what to reject. It's a matter of faith among editors that the best way to spot a book readers will like is to spot a book *they* like. The implicit assumption is that their preferences reflect those of readers. "If the book makes my eyes glaze over," observed editor-turned-agent Joni Evans, "it's probably going to do that to everyone else out there in the marketplace." Not necessarily. As opposed to even three or four decades ago, the tastes of those who buy manuscripts have drifted ever farther from the shore of those who buy books.

The best way to anticipate changing tastes of readers is to share those tastes. Historically, this has characterized the most successful editors and publishers. When an irate author asked Maxwell Perkins who he thought he was, Perkins responded that he thought of himself as "John Smith, U.S.A." Any self-respecting editor today would wince at the philistinism of such a cornball assertion, to say nothing of its presumption. This wasn't always so. Harper & Row's longtime publisher Cass Canfield took pride in being an "average" sort of person. "My likes and dislikes are those of the crowd," Canfield explained. Harper's publisher thought that "when an editor chooses a book because he figures out that it will appeal to a large popular audience, he usually guesses wrong. His only safeguard, in the exercise of literary judgment, is to have the kind of mind that shares the reaction of the crowd; what interests and amuses the mass book audience must be what interests and amuses him." How many editors today could, or would, make such a claim— even if they believed it to be true?

That's why consulting their own taste can be an unreliable barometer for editors of what will appeal to readers. Their own taste isn't necessarily shared by a mass audience. It can even be at variance. When an editor says, "No one's interested in shopping malls," what she's really saying is, "No one *I know* is interested in shopping malls." There's a difference. Conversely, when an editor reacts to a manuscript by saying, "Wow! I can really relate to this. This *speaks* to me!" she assumes that the same thing will be true of readers. It could be just the opposite.

In a smaller, less complex society, editors were not so removed from book buyers. The larger and more complicated society grows, the more we all seek solace in enclaves of "our kind." For pub people, this means that their gut reactions too often, unconsciously, reflect those of their tribe more than that of readers. Tom Wolfe has spent decades pointing out that the class bias inherent in publishing has kept its members from taking seriously important changes in popular culture that offend their sensibilities. Years ago, when Simon & Schuster editor Michael Korda tried to interest his colleagues in a manuscript he'd received in the mail about the country music business, he hit a brick wall. "If there was any subject less likely to cause enthusiasm at S & S than country music—except perhaps rodeo, cows, and crying women—I didn't know it," Korda wrote in his memoir, *Another Life*. Even though country music had gone mainstream with a vengeance in the rest of the country, that news hadn't reached publishing circles in New York. There, said Korda, "if it was noticed at all it was regarded with disdain."

Even when they take a flyer on writing that's distinctively from the great Out There, Manhattan-based pub people bring along their own propensities. After it was mentioned favorably in Jane and Michael Stern's *Road Food*, the Norske Nook in Osseo, Wisconsin, developed a cult following that included David Letterman, among others. In response, a major New York publisher asked its founder—Helen Myhre—to write a cookbook based on the comfort dishes she served at her midwestern café. After Myhre delivered a manuscript, her editor in New York said that certain changes were necessary. For one thing, she insisted that the author leave out her recipe for the popular Red Cherry Bars because it included maraschino cherries, a no-no in better eating circles. Miracle Whip was another taboo ingredient. Myhre was discouraged from using this dressing in her published recipes for potato salad and coleslaw as she did in those dishes at her restaurant. Myhre protested, saying, "Look it isn't only New York that is going to buy this book," to no avail. At her publisher's insistence she substituted homemade mayonnaise for Miracle Whip.

Does this all sound like discouraging news? It needn't. There are many astute pub people who resist the temptation to base their decisions on what pleases a small circle of literary friends. They read widely, with an emphasis on publications outside of

New York. The Internet is a godsend to them, with its wealth of information and perspectives. Traveling broadens their professional horizons (more than one has picked up a promising self-published title while on vacation and brought it home for republication). Attending writers' conferences in different parts of the country does the same thing.

Most of all, this type of pub person seeks out writers who are flying beneath their radar screen. Authors outside the publishing field of vision, she realizes, not only have manuscripts to offer but have *perspective*. Writers tend to share the taste of their readers in a way that few agents or editors do anymore. They are more likely to live among book buyers, see them at Starbucks, and discuss books with them in reading groups. This is true of published and unpublished writers alike. In addition to sharing their tastes, published authors have a close relationship with those who read their work. They see these readers at book signings. They speak to them at library programs. They hear from readers in letters and e-mail. They know what turns them on.

This gives writers at every level added value to publishers. Yourself, for example. Not only are you the source of pub people's product, you also have direct contact with their customers. Astute, open-minded agents and editors—the kind you'd like to work with—recognize your value to them precisely because you are outside their information loop and in intimate touch with book buyers. Even when they do compensate for their isolation with Net surfing and the like, what they cannot attain is what you possess: a *feel* for what's going on among readers, a *sense* of what's on the horizon where most book buyers live. Even if you are based in New York, but don't warm yourself at the publishing tribe's campfire, you have an outsider's perspective. In a business as haphazard as publishing, this makes you an unusually precious commodity.

Betting on Books

Publishing is a fundamentally unpredictable business. Often the only way to find out what will sell or not is by publishing the book.

James O'Shea Wade, editor

Without a gambling instinct and a taste for hazardous adventure a man should never hang out a publishing sign.

Cass Canfield, publisher

J. K. Rowling spent a year on welfare trying to interest editors in her novel about an otherworldly boy named Harry Potter. All returned it. So did a variety of agents whose names she found in directories. Since Rowling didn't have enough money to make photocopies, the single mother had to retype her manuscript when it became too dog-eared for continued submission. Why did no one see its potential? For starters, Rowling's novel was nearly twice as long as the typical book for young readers. It also seemed a bit *whimsical*. Smart agents knew that *Harry Potter* wasn't the sort of thing publishers were buying. The one who finally took it on was turned down by four more publishers before he wheedled an advance of $3,300 out of Bloomsbury Publishing in London.

Pub people may find episodes like J. K. Rowling's unnerving, but to writers they're encouraging. In general we can take comfort from the remarkable number of successful books that were rejected or neglected by publishers. This chapter includes a generous measure of such episodes. In and of themselves they signify nothing more than the fact that mistakes are made in any human endeavor. When it comes to publishing books, however, they also illustrate the inherent unpredictability of this pursuit. Publishing is essentially a business of guess and gamble. Outside of the latest *Harry Potter*, bringing a book to market is like introducing a new product. Will it be the latest Edsel or another PT Cruiser? Your guess is basically as good as anyone's. As a result, decisions about buying manuscripts and selling books are based to a surprising degree on gut reactions. "One makes an intuitive judgment," the head of a major publishing house told novelist Robert Oliphant, "after which one searches for reasons that will persuade one's colleagues the judgment is the act of a rational man."

Shooting Craps

Among themselves pub people routinely use the term *crapshoot* to depict what they do. Reading tastes evolve constantly, in ways that are nearly impossible to foresee. Predicting what will strike the fancy of readers has as much to do with selling short as selling toothpaste—maybe more. "A gamble and a sport," one editor called his vocation, saying that what he liked best about it was the sense of "action, high rolling, living on the edge."

Because it is such an unpredictable affair, publishing attracts those who are disposed to play hunches and trust their instincts. Sometimes this works out, sometimes it doesn't. The editor of John Jakes's first novel—*I, Barbarian*—didn't want to put the author's name on the jacket because he thought it sounded like a piece of machinery and was "unfit for big-scale stuff with a lot of action and romance." John Jakes's novels, full of action and romance, eventually sold over 50 million copies, all under his own name. The president of Warner Books had no problem with the author's name when he bought reprint rights to an upcoming Judith Krantz novel from Crown, but did want to change its title. "*Scruples* is a ridiculous title," he explained. "Nobody will know what it means. We've got to get Crown to change it." Crown didn't. As *Scruples*, Krantz's novel sold well over five million paperback copies.

Hit or miss, pub people *prefer* to consult their own predilections rather than study those of customers. Their market research consists primarily of "asking around the house" (i.e., soliciting each others' opinions). Many have a "Gloria" in their midst whom they consult, a clerical type whose taste they hope matches that of the reading public. Sales reps also bring news from the provinces about what books are being bought out there. But the news they bring is from independent booksellers, a shrunken group once removed from readers themselves. As a result, many pub people have only the vaguest idea of what's on their customers' minds. "It is a source of perpetual puzzlement to me to know why people buy our books," the venerable publisher Alfred A. Knopf once observed. So why don't pub people get out on the hustings and get to know their customers better? Lack of time. Inertia. Apprehension. "We are all a little afraid of the great world where people reach into their pockets for the money to buy a book," admitted one editor.

Conventional Wisdom, Publishing Division

Relying that much on their own judgment lends itself to developing conventional wisdom for assessing manuscripts and selling books. Like members of any tribe, pub people have fervent folk beliefs to which they cling until these beliefs are proven wrong. Then they develop new, equally fervent beliefs—which sometimes contradict the old ones. "Ice and snow does not go" was a popular publishing adage until books such as *Into Thin Air* and *Ice Bound* consigned this axiom to history's dustbin. Its replacement seemed to be "You can never get enough ice and snow." Other axiomatic flip-flops include:

- Men don't buy books (until Robert Bly's *Iron John*).
- Blacks don't buy books (until Terry McMillan's *Waiting to Exhale*).
- Country music fans don't buy books (until Loretta Lynn's *Coalminer's Daughter*).
- TV-watchers don't buy books (until Oprah's Book Club).
- Short-story collections don't sell (until Melissa Bank's *A Girl's Guide to Hunting and Fishing*).
- Books based on parables are non-starters (until *The One-Minute Manager* and *Who Moved My Cheese?*).

Such guidelines are usually based on how well previous books have done in the marketplace. This helps explain why new books are so often compared to old ones. ("In the tradition of," "Reminiscent of.") Sequels are the optimal genre for this way of thinking. That and series. (*The Dummies Guide to . . .*) Or knockoffs. (*The Complete Idiot's Guide to . . .*) An interesting statistical study would calculate how often the word *soul* has appeared in a book title since the unexpected success of *Care of the Soul*, or the word *light* since so many readers bought *Guided by the Light*.

Like most people in business, those in publishing are better at hiking blazed trails than they are at blazing new ones. As a result, manuscripts that might have sold yesterday are bought, ones that could sell tomorrow returned to sender. If an agent or editor thinks your idea isn't any good, that could mean you've sent them a bad idea. Or it could simply mean it doesn't resemble any book that has sold well in the past. Just because one publisher or many return your material, don't assume that their assessment of its prospects is the last word. They could be right. They might be wrong. They've been wrong often enough before.

The point is *not* that pub people don't know what they're doing. This simply isn't true. Publishing is filled with capable, shrewd individuals. Effective marketing campaigns devised by some helped make bestsellers of books such as *Latitude*, *Future Shock*, and *The World according to Garp*. But pub people as a group simply are not as omniscient as fledgling writers might imagine. "Surprise bestsellers" such as *Snow Falling on Cedars*, *The Road Less Traveled*, *Cold Mountain*, or *Secrets of the Ya-Ya Sisterhood* usually surprise their publishers as much as anyone. This makes for a high degree of uncertainty for those who buy manuscripts. "Given how many surprises there are on any given list," said one editor at a prominent trade house, "both good and bad, how well you are doing is often not known until you've done it."

On condition of anonymity, this longtime editor expanded on the vagaries of his vocation:

> An editor's judgments are always primarily subjective and include such extraneous factors as how long it's been since he last bought a book, his in-house status at the moment, or whether or not the book's agent is a hot one with whom he is desperate to do business. The editor can't really say these things out loud, however, so it's back to adopting the businesslike mode. But they are really in their business because of irrational passions, not because they are businesspeople. Editors tend to be of the "creative" type more than the business type, meaning they are usually high strung, sensitive, and insecure, just like writers.
>
> Yes, editors are practical and "sensible" with writers. If

they weren't, they wouldn't have jobs. Editors love talking to writers about the business of publishing, because there is no risk that they'll be found out. With writers they can make their statements seem sophisticated, worldly wise, and cynical, with no fear of contradiction. If anything, editors are more paranoid than writers, however, supremely insecure in their judgments—which after all are totally subjective. They are asked to make recommendations with often huge financial implications on the basis of a few pages of paper, and in the end, there is no sensible way to do that. So they spend most of their working days pretending to be something they are not, which is businesspeople. They struggle to find words to make their subjective, emotional opinions seem rational and financially sound.

The truth is that when it comes to predicting which books will succeed in the marketplace, pub people are close to clueless. That's the nature of their business. Outside of books written by a few brand-name authors, what readers will choose to buy is nearly impossible to anticipate. The year before *Angela's Ashes* and *The Liar's Club* were published, a Little, Brown editor assured me that the market for memoirs was so saturated that in the future, publishers wouldn't be able to *give* them away. Such examples of myopia may be a source of chagrin to pub people, but they're oddly encouraging to writers. Those who pass judgment on our work are, to say the least, fallible.

We Just Can't See It

When adman Theodor Geisel wrote a whimsical children's book in rhyme illustrated by himself, more than two dozen publishers turned it down. According to biographers Judith and Neil Morgan, Geisel was told that his book—called *A Story*

That No One Can Beat—differed too much from others on the market, that verse was out of fashion, and there was no market for fantasy. When the twenty-seventh publisher turned it down, Geisel carried his manuscript home with thoughts of burning it. On the way he bumped into a college classmate who had just become an editor in charge of children's books at the maverick Vanguard Press. After reading the manuscript, his classmate agreed to publish it if Geisel—writing as "Dr. Seuss"—could give him a snappier title. Geisel did: *And to Think That I Saw It on Mulberry Street.*

Geisel's experience was hardly unique:

- When songwriter Shel Silverstein decided to write a children's book, a Simon & Schuster editor sent the result back with this explanation: "Look, Shel, this *The Giving Tree* is O.K, but it falls between two stools—it ain't a kid's book and it ain't an adult one. I'm sorry, but I don't think you're going to find a publisher for it." *The Giving Tree* went on to sell more than 2 million copies for Harper & Row and launched Silverstein's career as one of history's bestselling authors of children's books.
- Harper & Row and Delacorte both rejected Mary Higgins Clark's first novel, *Where Are the Children?*—the latter from fear that its focus on children in jeopardy might upset women readers. After Simon & Schuster published her maiden novel, Clark became one of history's most successful authors, with a succession of novels that featured children in jeopardy.
- Seventeen publishers passed on Irving Stone's *Lust for Life.* Doubleday's sales department concluded that it couldn't sell a book about an unknown Dutch painter. An editor at another company dismissed Stone's manuscript as "a long, dull novel about an artist." After it was published

by Longmans, Green, Stone's fictionalized account of Vin-
cent van Gogh's life sold millions of copies.

• Because they thought readers were eager to forget about
World War II, Simon & Schuster and Knopf both rejected
Herman Wouk's *The Caine Mutiny* in 1949. Doubleday
finally published Wouk's future classic but couldn't get its
own book club—the Literary Guild—to offer his novel
to members. The Book-of-the-Month Club passed too. Its
judges didn't like the novel's love story.

• William Shirer could only coax a $10,000 advance from
Simon & Schuster for a book he'd spent a decade writing:
The Rise and Fall of the Third Reich. The publisher's sales
reps were dubious about its prospects. A small printing
was ordered. One Simon & Schuster editor advised Shirer
to find another line of work. His book on Hitler's Ger-
many went on to become one of history's all-time bestsellers.

• After two dozen publishers rejected Richard Bach's fable
about a freedom-loving bird, his agent told him, "Look,
they're not interested in a talking seagull." When Macmillan finally published *Jonathan Livingston Seagull*, it sold
more than 3 million copies in hardback. Popular Library
was offered the book's reprint rights, but passed. "*Jonathan
Livingston Seagull* will never make it as a paperback," its
publisher predicted. Avon reprinted Bach's book and sold
well over 8 million copies in paperback.

Such episodes provide yet another reason to accept frustration as part of the writing process, and not treat rebuffs as
terminal. Editors do make mistakes. The ideas they reject out
of hand today may be ones they're clamoring to buy tomorrow.
(As we'll see, this is sometimes literally true.) Because theirs is

such a guessing game, the word of a pub person is not necessarily the last one. In the crapshoot of publishing, decisions are too often based on obsolete information and outdated axioms. One of the ten editors who passed on *All the President's Men* assured its agent that "Washington books don't sell." A magazine editor declined an offer to serialize *Gone with the Wind* because it was a "period novel," adding that no one cared about the Civil War anymore. Such certitudes grow out of an implicit assumption that readers' tastes are static. They aren't. Other than novels by Danielle Steel and Stephen King, editors have little better idea than you or I do about what books readers will buy in the future. And bear in mind that three decades ago, when his name was unknown outside Durham, Maine, King himself submitted three chapters and an outline of a science fiction novel to a publisher. One month later it was returned with a note saying, "We are not interested in science fiction which deals with negative utopias. They do not sell."

That Won't Sell!

An editor once handed me a bound galley of a book on religious psychology that he was about to publish. I riffled its pages. The content looked awfully opaque. I handed it back with polite murmurs, thinking to myself, "This book will never sell." Its title was *Care of the Soul*.

No matter how confident their tone, whoever says of a proposed book, "It won't sell," is stating an opinion, not a verity. The only way to find out if a book will sell is to try to sell it. Trends have to start somewhere. Perhaps your project will start a trend, the one you've been told has no prospects in the marketplace. Others have been told the same thing:

- One of four editors to reject *Lolita* said of Vladimir Nabokov's novel, "It will not sell, and it will do immeasurable harm to a growing reputation."
- Among the many editors who returned John Grisham's first novel, *A Time to Kill*, one told his agent that readers had lost interest in books involving lawyers and trials.
- A first reader advised Little, Brown that Ayn Rand's *The Fountainhead* "won't sell." Bobbs-Merrill published this runaway bestseller, but fourteen years later returned the manuscript of Rand's *Atlas Shrugged*, calling it "unsaleable and unpublishable." A subsequent poll judged *Atlas Shrugged* the second most influential book in the history of American publishing.
- One publisher returned Pearl Buck's first novel, explaining that "the American public is not interested in anything on China."
- Before his first *The Making of the President* book appeared in 1960 and became a huge bestseller that kicked off a series, Theodore White was warned repeatedly by publishers that readers had no interest in presidential campaigns once they were over.
- An editor returned the manuscript of Jean Auel's subsequent bestseller *The Clan of the Cave Bear* with the explanation that, since she wasn't a big-name author like James Michener, he didn't think they'd be able to sell very many copies of her novel.
- Laurence Peter's *The Peter Principle* was returned by thirty editors. "I can foresee no commercial possibilities for such a book and consequently can offer no encouragement," one told the author. When it finally sold, Peter's book about his principle became a mega-bestseller.
- William Kennedy's Pulitzer Prize–winning *Ironweed* was

rejected by thirteen publishers. Their prevailing opinion was that no one wanted to read about bums in Albany.

- Elie Wiesel's agent couldn't sell his autobiographical novel *Night* to a major New York publisher. "We have certain misgivings as to the size of the American market [for Wiesel's novel]," explained a Scribner editor. Four decades after it was published by Hill & Wang, *Night* still sells several thousand copies a year.

- A reader's report dismissed Bernard Malamud's *The Assistant* as "superficial and unconvincing. . . . I do not see this book as a very well told story on any level. I do not think it would have either a good critical reception or substantial sales."

- The British publisher W. H. Allen turned down Frederick Forsyth's *Day of the Jackal* as having "no reader interest."

Rhymes and Reasons

Most editors say they can usually tell within a page, a paragraph, even a sentence or two, whether a submission is publishable. To a large degree this makes perfect sense. Too much of what they're sent is badly written, incoherent, uncommercial, or all three. But in some cases an editor may simply have stopped reading too soon. More than once editors have upbraided agents for not sending them a manuscript that became a bestseller, only to be told they *had* been sent that manuscript, but returned it. In such cases the editor probably hadn't read enough of the submission to make a memorable impression.

André Gide, who called his rejection of *Remembrance of Things Past* the biggest mistake he ever made as an editor, in a subsequent letter of apology confessed to Marcel Proust that he'd only given his manuscript a cursory look. After reading the book when it was finally published by a competitor, Gide said that not reading Proust's manuscript more carefully was one of his life's "most burning regrets."

Gide's blunder to the contrary, superior manuscripts usually aren't hard to spot, even at a glance. But there are only so many superior manuscripts to go around. Publishers must fill their catalogs with new titles every season, and most slots are assigned to books of varying quality. It's with the middling manuscripts that editors earn their pay. These confront them with the most challenging task of all: making up their minds.

Agent Colleen Mohyde, who was once an editor at Little, Brown, told me that in both cases her job was to read submissions, form an opinion, then act based on her opinion. I thought this was an unusually perceptive and accurate depiction of how publishing decisions are made. That's basically all any agent or editor does, really—form opinions and act on opinions—even though they often portray this activity in loftier terms.

This helps explain why some books get published and others don't with so little apparent rhyme or reason. Even the plausible fraction of submissions editors read may not suit the needs of their employer, or their own tastes, or literary fashion. That's where the potential for mischief is greatest. It's why—even when many negative reactions to a submission of yours converge—you shouldn't leap to the conclusion that your work lacks merit. This could be the case. But it might not be. It could simply be one more case of an agent or editor conveying tribal folk wisdom or making a snap judgment they'll live to regret. The best of them are more aware of this danger than anyone. When she was president of Putnam, Phyllis Grann was renowned for her ability to spot future bestsellers. But Grann freely admitted to getting it wrong on a regular basis. "Every year there is a book on the lists that is killing me," said Grann, "because I was so stupid that I didn't think it would work."

Categorical Imperatives

After *The Bridges of Madison County* came out of nowhere (Iowa, actually) to become a blockbuster hit, St. Martin's editor Bob Wyatt confessed that if Robert James Waller's manuscript had landed on his desk, he would have returned it. His reasons? "Too short. Not enough audience appeal. It didn't fit any category and it couldn't be compared to anything." A few years later *The Christmas Box*—which enjoyed such enormous success as a self-published title, then on Simon & Schuster's list—was initially turned down by dozens of publishers because it was, among other things, "uncategorizable."

Category is a very important concept in publishing. Exactly what does that mean? Visit any bookstore, a large one especially, and note the headings under which books are shelved. If you can easily determine where your book would be placed, it fits into an existing category. If you can't, you have a problem, at least as far as publishers and booksellers are concerned. Earlier we discussed the confusion of publishers as they tried to categorize *Animal Farm*. After George Orwell's novel was published, this proved to be a problem for booksellers as well, leading its author to tour London bookstores, moving his book from the children's section to one for adults.

The need to categorize is entirely understandable. Without categories booksellers would shelve books in anarchic confusion, and clerks wouldn't know where to direct customers. ("You might try a few feet over that way.") Faced with a multitude of titles in the marketplace, the human mind craves order, definition, categories. At the same time, an overemphasis on categorization is a key factor limiting publishers' ability to see beyond their headlights.

It would take inhuman foresight and resolve to turn away from categories of books that are selling briskly and look for new ones altogether. Yet this is the only real way to stay ahead of breaking waves. Publishers recognize that the types of books buyers crave today may gather dust in two or three years' time. What's harder to anticipate is how entire categories themselves may change. Guidance is as likely to come from without as within: from authors, say, or booksellers.

Two decades ago, an independent sales representative persuaded B. Dalton and Waldenbooks to *create* a new book category by simply reorganizing their stores' shelves. What the rep got these chains to do was move all their books related to "recovering" that were now scattered within psychology, sociology, and self-help sections to a new section called *Recovery*. That was a daring departure from the norm because it risked alienating browsers who might not want to be seen in this section. The bookstores' category-creation had just the opposite effect, however. Readers flocked to the shelves labeled *Recovery*, and sales of books in that new category skyrocketed.

Publishers are always scrambling to foresee not only the next big book but the next big category. They realize that today's categories may not survive changing tastes. Old ones will wither, new ones sprout. Once you've determined which categories of book will interest future readers, it's easier to sign up books that fit them. But what will those categories be?

The best way to find out is to publish books that are hard to categorize. Books by pathbreakers such as George Orwell and J. K. Rowling didn't fit easily into predetermined slots. That's in the nature of those who break paths. In recent years mainstream publishers have been forced by determined writers such as Terry McMillan, E. Lynn Harris, and Zane to face the fact that a whole new category—mainstream fiction based on African-American characters—catered to a market they didn't even know existed. As we'll discuss more fully in chapter 10, all of those authors were told by publishers that there was "no market" for their books. What this really meant was that they didn't fit into any category publishers knew how to reach.

When publishers say, "There's no market for such-and-such a book," they're usually right, with regard to *existing* markets. On the other hand, new markets—big ones—are out there waiting to be tapped. There are readers not being served because publishers don't know how to reach them (i.e., how to go beyond existing categories and create new ones).

That's where authors come in. If your writing can deliver a new audience to a publisher, you are gold (only they may not realize it—yet). Our very best ideas may be the ones that editors reject out of hand, not necessarily because they're bad but because they're too far outside their frame of reference. This has always been true. "I think the percentage of very good books—the really notable books—that are declined is higher than the percentage of the highly competent mediocrities," said Maxwell Perkins. "The reason is that the books of the greatest talent are almost always full of trouble, and difficult, and they do not conform to the usual standards."

The best books don't fit easily into existing market slots; they forge new ones. This is extremely difficult to do in an environment built around current categories. Yet the very difficulty presented by category-busters can be a sign of their potential. "When you have a book that intrigues you, but is not like other books, that's a clue to be very interested," said editor-turned-book doctor Gerald Sindell, who signed up the future number one bestseller *Ladies of the Club* for a pittance when he was at Putnam because no other publisher wanted it. "The resistance will be fierce—it won't fit pattern recognition needs of your associates, the sales force, the book buyers, or your publisher. But you are looking at opportunity. The big books are, generally, the hardest. To be involved with a best-seller, you need to be a contrarian in your gut."

All of this is by way of saying, if agents or publishers return your submissions, they aren't necessarily making the right decision—on their own terms. When they say, "It won't sell," they could be right, or they could be wrong. Certainly they're correct in using the present tense because all they are saying is that it won't sell today. What will sell tomorrow is anyone's guess. If you can hang on long enough to find a visionary editor, or for the publishing tides to turn, your day may come.

This is easier said than done, however. It helps to have support from those I call *encouragers*. As we'll see, there are lots of them out there. The fact that there are those who encourage them is just one of many reasons that writers find the wherewithal to keep on writing. Let's consider some.

{ III }

BEYOND FRUSTRATION

· 8 ·

Encouragers

However tough the peasant in his heart, every writer
needs people who believe in him, give him a shoulder to
cry on, and value what he values.

John Gardner

So many people took an interest in my work early on
and encouraged me that I almost can't believe my good
luck.

Ann Beattie

Early in her career Eudora Welty got the letter every fledgling
writer dreams of getting. Diarmuid Russell, a literary agent in
New York, had heard promising reports about Welty from an
editor at Doubleday. Might he represent her? "Yes—," she
responded, "be my agent." The two worked together for more
than three decades, until Russell's death in 1973. With her
agent's help, Eudora Welty eventually became such a literary
icon that we forget how many years she spent having each and
every story returned from publishers big and small. During this
discouraging period, the continued reassurance of Diarmuid
Russell was virtually the only thing that kept her writing. A
few months after signing up with him, and before he had sold
any of her stories, Welty wrote Russell, "That there are people
like you . . . in the world fills me with the most opposite feeling
to discouragement." In the midst of a long, frustrating period

when the Mississippian was considered only a regional author of middling promise, Russell kept his client's spirits up. "I am sorry I can't send you money yet," Russell wrote her at one point, "or give you good news but all I can say is don't worry, for anyone who writes as well as you do is certain to be all right." Russell repeatedly assured his author that it was just a matter of time before her talent was recognized. And he was right. Their relationship grew so close that an entire book has been written about it: *Author and Agent*, by Michael Kreyling.

Like Welty, successful writers routinely cite specific individuals—friends, colleagues, teachers, spouses, agents, editors—who at some critical juncture gave them the reassurance they needed to keep writing. I call these people *encouragers*. Especially when your work hasn't been published and you have no idea if it ever will be published, encouragers are invaluable. They are the benign twin of *discouragers*, the kindly Jekyll to those folks' disparaging Hyde. Encouragers can be found in many guises and in unexpected places. Jay Parini got encouragement from the affable patrons of Lou's Diner in Hanover, New Hampshire, where he wrote three books, and from the restaurant's owner himself. "I don't think any would have made it into print without Lou's hospitality," said Parini. When she was an office clerk with a novel in the works, Terry McMillan found encouragement in the radio studio of Irwin Gonshak, a retired schoolteacher in Flushing, Queens, who hosted a weekly hour-long show devoted to aspiring writers. A therapist gave E. Lynn Harris the reassurance he needed to leave his job as a computer salesman and write full-time. During the harrowing years when he struggled to write his first novel, John Grisham got a boost from Donald Zacharias, the president emeritus of his alma mater—Mississippi State University—who not only encouraged the young lawyer but said the university would be proud to archive and display his papers. That promise was kept in the form of the John Grisham Room at Mississippi State.

Many writers contend that writing is inherently lonely and frustrating. If you can't put up with the isolation and the aggravation, they say, sell Tupperware. While it's true that no one can hold the hands that write, there are many hours of the day when a writer's hands are free to be held. Just because you need to *write* alone doesn't mean you always need to *be* alone, physically or spiritually. Writers need solace, encouragement, and support as much as anyone, maybe more.

During my own three decades of writing, I've been helped by a changing cast of invaluable encouragers. Early on, the support of relatives and friends was paramount. Since I didn't study the subject, I can't point to any writing teachers who encouraged me, but my first boss out of college—a newspaper publisher—was a vital source of psychic support. His belief that I had a promising future helped me believe that too. After becoming a freelance writer, I sought the counsel of several editors at a trade magazine published near my home, partly for their expertise, even more for the reassurance I needed so badly, and they were generous enough to give. (It helped that, even though they knew their craft, these editors were not in a position to accept or reject my work.) Members of writers' groups to which I belonged at that time offered both helpful critiques of my writing and reminders that I was indeed a writer. My agent, and the man who edited three of my first four books, did the same thing. Although I haven't worked with that editor for two decades, he's remained an important source of support, even offering to comment on writing of mine that's being published elsewhere. Other encouragers I acquired along the way included friends, a publisher's consultant, a retired editor, a talk show host who once interviewed me on television, and various colleagues. For several years my wife, Muriel, doubled as both an encourager and critiquer. Muriel has largely retired from the latter position but still fills the former.

Encouragers come from many walks of life, not always obvious ones, and change over time. At the outset, family, friends, and teachers are paramount. Later, colleagues and spouses step in. Along the way, sundry merchants and psychologists may fill that role. Ultimately, with luck, it's taken over by agents and editors. Finding the right encouragers at the right time is one of the developing writer's most important tasks.

Family

When I got home from grade school, my mother greeted me with hugs and cookies, then sat me beside her at the dining room table so we each could "write." She scribbled stories and poems in a spiralbound notebook with her mechanical pencil. I wrote with crayon on newsprint. This is where I first got the idea that perhaps I could be a writer. Later, Mom had the grace to swallow her disappointment and show only her pride when I began to publish the kinds of books she'd hoped to publish but didn't.

No encouragement can match a parent's. This gives writers a solid foundation from which to launch their career. Mary Higgins Clark's mother gave her a journal to write in when she was six, then urged young Mary to read her poems aloud. "Mary has written a lovely new poem today," Mrs. Higgins would tell visiting relatives and friends. "She has promised to recite it for us. Mary, stand on the landing and recite your lovely new poem." When her daughter had finished reciting, Mrs. Higgins led the applause, then assured everyone present that "Mary is going to be a successful writer when she grows up." Even at her most discouraged, Mary Higgins Clark wrote in her memoir, *Kitchen Privileges*, when all her stories were coming back by return mail, she never lost hope. Her mother's "absolute vote of confidence," with its conviction that she would make it, gave Clark the assurance that she would—as she did.

Stephen King got similar support from his mother. When King began writing stories at age twelve, his mother gave him the forty or fifty cents he needed for stamps to send them to publishers when she was denying herself food due to extreme poverty. King later called his mother's backing "steady and unwavering." That support kept him going through his scores of rejected stories and novels until *Carrie* was finally bought by Doubleday.

King was lucky to have not only a supportive mother but, later, a supportive wife. The horror writer has taken every opportunity to say that without his wife's backing he doubts that he'd have kept writing. It was Tabitha King who pulled from a wastebasket the discarded pages that went on to become *Carrie*. This was in the tradition of George Orwell's friend Mabel Fierz, who ignored his instructions to throw away the much-rejected manuscript for *Down and Out in Paris and London* but save the paper clips. Samuel Beckett's wife-to-be, Suzanne Deschevaux-Dumesnil, flogged his early work from publisher to publisher when he was too discouraged to do anything but brood in Parisian cafés. "I owe everything to Suzanne," Beckett later wrote. "She was the one who went to see the publishers while I used to sit in a café 'twiddling my fingers' or whatever it is one twiddles."

Long after they divorced, Alice Munro said that without the support of her first husband she could not have become a writer. There was a time, Munro explained, when the only form of recognition she got was the fact that her husband thought she had potential. "Without that," said Munro, "I couldn't have survived." Mary McCarthy said she would never have become a writer had her new husband—the critic Edmund Wilson— not told her she had a fiction-writing gift and stuck her in a room that had a desk, paper, and some writing implements, with instructions not to emerge until she'd written something. McCarthy did as she was told. The story she wrote in that room—later published in *Southern Review* and included in her collection *The Company She Keeps*—was the first one McCarthy had ever written.

Most of us are not married to the likes of an Edmund Wilson, alas. That's why, past a certain stage, it is risky to seek encouragement from one's family or spouse. They're too prone to think your writing is wonderful because they think you're wonderful. When someone who cares for you reads a piece of your work and says, "I love this," what he or she usually means is, "I love you." There's a difference.

An important distinction must be made between yourself as a person and as a writer. I seek spiritual support from some to whom I never show my work, and offer that support to others whose work I never read. I have friends who love me and encourage me as a writer but don't particularly care for my writing. (I've never considered liking my writing to be a test of friendship.) That kind of unconditional support is great to get as a person, but not from someone who is in a position to evaluate your work. When it comes to writing professionally, blind support can be worse than none at all. Taking your writing seriously means showing it to encouragers who can also assess its quality.

Teachers

Novelist Stephen Cannell said he owes his career not only to the doubters who goaded him as a young dyslexic but to a writing teacher at the University of Oregon who looked past his misspellings and gave him "encouragement and hope."

As Cannell discovered, teachers can be a source of informed encouragement. Unlike friends and family, teachers are more likely to combine support of aspiring writers with a critical assessment of their work. At the same time, they don't have to be as tough-minded as editors making bottom-line judgments. Teachers serve the same function for fledgling writers that half-way houses serve for released prisoners: easing them into the skeptical world beyond. Some are renowned for making strenuous efforts to help their students get published. Muriel Rukeyser, who taught Alice Walker poetry-writing at Sarah Lawrence, herself sent Walker's poems to the *New Yorker*. Even though they weren't accepted, this gave Walker the validation she needed to keep writing. Later, Rukeyser helped Walker find an agent, and a publisher for her first book of poems.

In some ways, getting encouragement from teachers is the most valuable part of studying writing. Beneficiaries of their largesse invariably cite the psychic support of such teachers more than any professional pointers. Scott Turow gave Tillie Olsen enormous credit for simply taking his work seriously when she taught him at Amherst. Novelist Molly Gloss (*Wild Life*) found the writing course she took from Ursula Le Guin at Portland State University "life altering," because it was the first time someone she respected so much said to her, "You are a writer."

Although she once claimed that her undergraduate writing teachers specialized in hand-holding and chin-tickling, Ann Patchett later wrote an essay in which she paid tribute to Sarah Lawrence professor Allan Gurganus. Gurganus, said Patchett, not only taught her 90 percent of what she knew about writing fiction but later became her mentor and, more than that, her model of a writer whose life was well lived. Mentors like him are extremely hard to come by, she observed, because the generous ones may have little to teach, while the brilliant ones might rather keep their insights to themselves. Gurganus was an exception who combined generosity with profound writing ability of his own. "To have received some genuine guidance in my life," Patchett wrote, more than a decade after leaving Sarah Lawrence, "to have received it at a time when I was capable of listening in a way I probably no longer am, was a great gift."

Mentors

Like Gurganus, many teachers double as mentors for students and former students. But they are not the only source of mentoring. Jay Parini had one important mentor relationship with his teacher Alastair Reid, and another with Robert Penn Warren, whom he sought out as a fan. Parini found the importance of the mentor-mentee relationship even greater than that of teacher-student. His mentors didn't just assess his work and suggest where to send it; they educated him "by the example of their life or their work or some mixture of the two." Long after Warren died, Parini found himself reflecting on work habits he'd observed in the older poet-novelist, and hearing echoes of his counsel.

Over time this relationship can get dicey, however. Since it involves two people working in the same field—potential competitors—the mentor-mentee relationship is more complex than that of teacher-student. For one thing, a colleague-mentor isn't paid to encourage, as teachers are. For another, if a full-time writer, he or she is likely to lack social grace. And there is always the risk that a mentee will do well and be seen as a rival. Encouragement then can get mingled with subtle discouragement. The support offered by colleague-mentors can sometimes be hard to distinguish from the criticism of discouragers. An important task of the writer-in-process is to recognize this fact and to pan golden flecks of encouragement from the dull sand of disparagement.

Encouragers sometimes come disguised as discouragers. Two important encouragers in my own early career were magazine editors who rejected submissions of mine but went on to become friends and supporters. That parallels the experience of J. T. LeRoy with novelist and short-story writer Mary Gaitskill. LeRoy was befriended by Gaitskill, who critiqued his early work. The aspiring young fiction writer found this friendship encouraging and discouraging at once: encouraging because Gaitskill had so much faith in his ability; discouraging because she didn't hesitate to criticize LeRoy's work. Gaitskill minced no words when doing this. In response, LeRoy for a time felt too discouraged to write at all. But he never doubted that his published colleague—who also gave LeRoy stories by Nabokov and Flannery O'Connor with suggestions on what to look for when reading them—was actually trying to help him. "She was very, very encouraging," said LeRoy, who went on to publish his own fiction.

Colleagues

Colleagues can double as encouragers, and often do. F. Scott Fitzgerald was renowned for the help he offered young writers, including Ernest Hemingway. Nor was Fitzgerald threatened by colleagues, even successful ones. "He did not regard writing as competitive and did not resent the success of other writers," noted his biographer, Matthew Bruccoli.

The same thing can be said of many contemporary writers. E. Lynn Harris cited not only his therapist but Maya Angelou as an important source of early support. Long after she became a literary luminary, Ann Beattie recalled the helpful and reassuring response to her work by colleagues she called "loyal first readers." Beattie also got a phone call out of the blue from Donald Barthelme after her second story appeared in the *New Yorker*, and a fan letter from Anne Tyler. Writers such as Stephen King and Elinor Lipman are renowned for their willingness to help colleagues. "For as long as I live," one author wrote Lipman in thanks for a blurb, "I will never forget that you went out of your way to help my first novel."

As we've seen, authors routinely cite each other in their books' acknowledgments. Some have even dedicated books to colleagues. Essayist bell hooks dedicated *sisters of the yam* to Toni Cade Bambara. Early in hooks's career, when others were disparaging her efforts and saying there was no market for books by black women, hooks got steadfast support from author-editor Bambara. "When other folks rebuked and scorned me," hooks wrote in *remembered rapture*, "Toni would respond by writing the encouraging letter—making the don't-let-it-get-you-down phone call."

There are times when that type of encouragement from a colleague can be the only thing that keeps a writer writing. Cynthia Ozick said this is especially crucial for young writers whose only form of recognition is "private publication through friends." But it isn't just neophytes who find private publication invaluable. Philip Roth sent nearly completed manuscripts to selected critiquers whose judgment he respected, including the woman who interviewed him for *Paris Review*. Gail Godwin and John Irving mailed each other drafts of their work for years after they met at the Iowa Writers' Workshop. Even after winning his Nobel, Saul Bellow routinely circulated work-in-progress among colleagues. Bellow sought help and friendship from other writers throughout his career and wondered why more authors didn't support each other this way.

Literary history includes close friendships among writers who did give each other crucial support: Henry James and Edith Wharton, Samuel Beckett and James Joyce, Anne Sexton and Maxine Kumin, Eudora Welty and Katherine Anne Porter, Herman Melville and Nathaniel Hawthorne. When Melville met Hawthorne, he immediately sensed that his older colleague was a man who might encourage him. And Hawthorne was. After Hawthorne read a manuscript of *Moby Dick*, Melville wrote his friend-colleague: "A sense of unspeakable security is in me at this moment on account of your having understood the book." He then dedicated the novel to Nathaniel Hawthorne. In time Hawthorne came to feel that his younger colleague was crowding him and put some distance in their friendship. But it was one Melville considered instrumental to his growth as a novelist.

Like mentor-mentee relationships, those among colleagues can be complex: supportive in some cases, disparaging in others, or both at once. In a book on four literary friendships, including that of Melville and Hawthorne, David Laskin observed that "each vibrated between frequencies of love and jealousy, support and resentment, reverence and disgust, admiration and anger, passion and skepticism, idealism and disappointment." So it goes in friendships between writers. There are lots of cross-currents here. T. S. Eliot allowed Ezra Pound to substantially revise *The Wasteland*, then inscribed Pound's copy with a backhanded tribute to him as *il miglior fabbro* (a phrase from Dante's *Purgatoria* meaning "the better craftsman"). Colleagues can be too ambivalent about each other to offer unalloyed support. It was said of Hemingway that he could only befriend another writer if he felt certain that writer would never be his equal. Hemingway was notorious for trying to undercut any writer who threatened him, especially F. Scott Fitzgerald, despite Fitzgerald's support of him when Hemingway was an unknown.

Apparently, some writers are simply too arrogant to be of much use to colleagues. This is usually just a facade, of course. Writers tend to be preternaturally shy, and arrogance is a capital disguise for shyness. That's true of men especially, many of whom engage in a lot of chest pounding and hoo-ha about writers being the last of the Lone Rangers. Women seem more receptive to the idea that writers might help each other. Mary Gordon has said that the best part of being a woman writer has been the companionship of others like her. "I think it is lonelier to be a man writer than a woman writer now," Gordon observed, "because I do not think that men are as good at being friends to one another as women are. Perhaps, since they have not thought they needed each other's protection, as women have known we have needed each other's, they have not learned the knack of helpful, rich concern which centers on a friend's work. They may be worried, since they see themselves as hewers of wood and slayers of animals, about production, about the kind of achievement that sees its success only in terms of another's failure. They may not be as kind to one another; they may not know how."

This is hardly true across the board. Terry McMillan credited Ishmael Reed with encouragement that kept her going early on, as Ann Patchett did with Allan Gurganus. I've dealt with women who were as scathing as Don Rickles, and men who were as nurturing as Florence Nightingale. The editor I've found most supportive is a husky six-footer who could easily intimidate me if he chose to. My first agent was an overbearing woman who stood four-foot-ten but loomed like Wilt Chamberlain in my cowed imagination.

Agents

At some point, the reassurance of family, friends, teachers, mentors, and colleagues isn't enough. Then writers want to hear that their work has merit, that it might even be worth publishing, by someone who doesn't know them, who doesn't even know what they look like. Visions of agents begin to dance in their head. Perhaps that person will be like a literary personal trainer, a coach who can hold their hand and prepare them to storm the barricades of publishing.

Because writers work alone, with so little in the way of encouragement, the prospect of *an agent* can take on mythic proportions. To a desperate writer (i.e., nearly anyone who writes), the proverbial agent looms like an angel come to rescue them from raging floodwaters. A common fantasy among aspiring writers is that once they're in the hands of a shrewd, nurturing literary representative, they'll be on their way to a glorious, high-morale literary career. I think that is what's behind the question fledgling writers so often ask published ones: "How can I get an agent?"

As we saw with Eudora Welty, there are grounds for the good-agent fantasy. An agent such as Diarmuid Russell can be a first-rate encourager. Mary Higgins Clark was so grateful to her agent that she named one of her daughters after her. Any number of authors have dedicated books to their agent. In *The Joy Luck Club*, Amy Tan acknowledged hers "for saving my life." Alice Munro dedicated *Selected Stories* to the agent she called, "My essential support and friend for twenty years." Other authors who have dedicated books to agents include Bernard Malamud, Ken Follett, Frederick Busch, and Andrew Greeley. Norman Mailer twice included his agent in book dedications.

Agents wear different hats at different times for different

clients. Parent-figure. Bodyguard. Boss. Confidant. Therapist. Matchmaker. (Writers James Carroll and Alexandra Marshall were introduced by their agent, a part-time Episcopal priest who represented them both and subsequently married them.) A few writers have even married their agents. This relationship can be intense. Joe McGinnis told me that leaving his first agent was harder than leaving his first wife.

All of this is by way of saying that yes, under the right circumstances an agent can be an outstanding encourager. The dream of agent as shrewd soul mate, a combination of Jack Welch and Mister Rogers, is not without foundation. But for most writers and aspiring writers, the reality is more complicated.

Even though having an agent "take you on" is among the most encouraging moments in a writing career, it can be deceptive. Just because one adds you to her list of clients doesn't mean she has the time to nurture your career, lift your spirits, or considers holding authors' hands part of her job. Nor should she, necessarily. Nurture is not what every agent is good at. True, some can be as reassuring as Mother Teresa, but others can be as caustic as Nurse Ratched. (Recall the agent who told Charles Baxter that she *hated* his first novel.)

A need for encouragement is not reason enough to contact agents. Hand-holding is not their primary job. Their primary job is representing clients' work. To do this, agents need publishable manuscripts. Up to a point, they're willing to hold clients' hands to get them. Too many writers want their hand held first, however, manuscript to follow. Their priorities are reversed. Agents are best queried when one needs *representation* and is ready for it; not because one's morale needs boosting. The bane of agents' lives is hearing from writers whose work has been pulled from the oven before it's fully baked. This doesn't necessarily mean they're bad writers; just not prepared ones. "I am a believer in not showing anything until you're ready," said agent Noah Lukeman, "which is why I don't have that much patience for first novelists who show their work after three months and then are angry if I turn it down."

The paradox is that an agent can best help you when you no longer *need* his or her help. In other words, once you are writing publishable material, an agent can help get it to the right editor for the right price, on the best terms. If your writing is not ready to be published, however, an agent can do little for you. She is a *broker*, not a teacher or a counselor. Therefore, any agent will be most receptive to your query once you have at least a bit of a track record, a few things published, to encourage her. Like writers, agents need reassurance too. So, yes, by all means seek representation, but don't do so prematurely. Premature representation can be worse than no representation at all.

Suppose you do feel ready for prime time and query agents, only to be turned down. If so, you have lots of company— distinguished company. Any number of successful authors were rejected in multiples by agents who now rue the day. Like editors, agents make mistakes on a regular basis. Twenty-four of them declined to represent Nicholas Sparks before the one who did got him a $1-million advance from Warner for *The Notebook*. Sue Harrison said that sixteen agents passed on *Mother Earth Father Sky*, her novel that made lots of money for the agent who took it on. Stuart Krichevsky, who represented *The Perfect Storm* and *In the Heart of the Sea*, said of his worst day as agent, "I distinctly remember my head hitting the breakfast table when I read that HarperCollins had paid over a million dollars for a self-published book I'd turned down—*Mutant Message Down Under*."

In addition:

- An agent to whom Danielle Steel submitted her first novel, *Going Home*, advised the aspiring author to go home and have more children, since her writing would never sell. The agent who *did* take her on got rich on Steel's subsequent success. (Danielle Steel is the only woman among the top six bestselling American authors.)
- After reading part of Susanna Moore's novel *My Old Sweetheart*—which went on to be nominated for a National Book Award—a prestigious agent suggested Moore consider another line of work.
- Just before James Michener won the Pulitzer Prize for *Tales from the South Pacific* and catapulted into the ranks of bestselling authors, his agent decided Michener had so few prospects in the marketplace that he ended their relationship.
- When he showed his then-agent the manuscript for *Ishmael*, Daniel Quinn said the agent warned him that no publisher was interested in "that kind of world-saving thing." At last count the publisher who disagreed had sold more than 600,000 copies of Quinn's novel.

By recounting these episodes, I'm not trying to denigrate agents or to suggest that writers are better off without them. To the contrary. I don't even want to *look* at a book contract that an agent hasn't vetted. A good agent can be an author's best single source of counsel, guidance, and support. Some writers hit the Eudora Welty jackpot and get an agent such as Diarmuid Russell. Like any literary representative, though, even Russell was in business to make a living. Most agents aren't averse to making a good living. This doesn't make them avaricious. If wealth were their only goal, there are more lucrative, less speculative ways to get rich. Discovering writers, helping writers, then advocating on their behalf are what really turn them on (most of them, anyway). As editors move from house to house, agents have become the constant in their clients' lives. As publishers downsize and lay off editorial staff, agents are more important than ever as writers' first readers. Many editors prefer not to consider a manuscript that hasn't been prescreened by an agent. You can feel far more confident that an agent *will* open your envelope and take a look at what's inside—even a piece of writing from someone they've never heard of. "Whenever I opened an unsolicited manuscript," said one agent, "there was this tremendous excitement of tearing it open and wondering, 'Is this it?' "

Editors

Maxwell Perkins was thought to have been the brains behind Thomas Wolfe's early novels, the one who edited them to a fare-thee-well and perhaps even did some discreet rewriting. The editor himself said that his principal contribution to Wolfe's work lay in the realm of his author's spirit. According to Perkins, the main thing he did for Wolfe was "keeping him from losing belief in himself by believing in him." He succeeded. Wolfe dedicated *Of Time and the River* to Maxwell Perkins, "who stuck to the writer of this book through times of bitter hopelessness and doubt and would not let him give in to his own despair."

Like Perkins, some editors are famous for their sympathetic treatment of writers. Such editors reassure anxious writers, boost their spirits, soothe their nerves. One editor of mine said her most important task was simply *listening* to her authors when they were discouraged. Joan Didion depicted the way editor Henry Robbins dealt with her as "almost parental." Didion dedicated a book to him. Quite a few other authors have dedicated books to editors. In the preface to her *Collected*

Stories, Mavis Gallant said she owed everything to William Maxwell—her *New Yorker* editor for twenty-five years. The first time they met, Gallant explained, she was a young ex-journalist who had fled Montreal for Paris to write fiction. "He asked just a few questions," Gallant recalled, "and let me think it was perfectly natural to throw up one's job and all one's friends and everything familiar and go thousands of miles away to write. He made it seem no more absurd or unusual than taking a bus to visit a museum. Everyone else I knew had quite the opposite to say; I felt suddenly like a stranded army with an unexpected ally."

After his mother and wife, King is most effusive in crediting Doubleday editor William Thompson for his "kindness" when King was an unknown young writer sending him submission after submission, and getting letters of encouragement in response. These were not letters of acceptance, at first, but ones that promised to give his work a fair hearing. To King that was "everything." King stayed in touch with Thompson through several crushing turndowns until they clicked on *Carrie*. Thompson himself later noted, "Oddly enough, the rejections strengthened our personal connection."

This is why it's so very important to read between the lines of rejection letters. Even editors who return submissions can prove to be encouragers. Robert Olen Butler—who later won a Pulitzer Prize—took heart from the twenty editors who passed on his first novel because so many of them praised the book. Writers must be receptive to this sort of support, however. When you're smarting from the sting of rejection, it's easy to overlook. Novelist Luanne Rice got so discouraged early in her career that she stopped opening manila envelopes returning stories she'd sent to magazines, and therefore didn't even see the encouraging notes many editors had included. Had Rice done so, her stalled career might have got on track sooner.

All rejection is not the same. When you get responses that sound discouraging from those in a position to know, don't throw them away and book a flight to Katmandu. Give it a few days and review their message. It might have been a helpful one, an embrace in the form of a rebuff.

After Larry Brown's editor read the third draft of a novel he was writing, she told the Mississippi novelist that it began on page 160. What could be more discouraging? Brown resolved to trash it. His editor talked him out of doing this, however. "You've worked by yourself all this time," she told Brown. "You haven't had any guidance. I understand all of that. But this is too good an idea for you to throw away. Just trust me and work on it with me. I'm going to help you." She was right. Larry Brown found that this editor not only kept his spirits up but taught him much about writing fiction that eventually resulted in his much-improved novel *Dirty Work*.

Brown had the wisdom to see the encouragement that lay beneath his editor's criticism. Experienced writers realize that these two can't always be cleaved so cleanly. They understand that editors must critique with one hand, encourage with the other (or at least try not to discourage). One task takes objectivity, the other empathy. That's a hard combination to pull off. Compounding this challenge is the fact that authors are only one in a constellation of parties whom editors must try to satisfy. Within their office they belong to a pecking order that includes publishers, marketing directors, colleague-competitors, and many others. At best they can only keep one eye on authors, while keeping the other trained on their flanks.

Appearances to the contrary, editors were not put on this earth to make writers miserable. They just have priorities of their own, ones that sometimes converge with those of writers and sometimes don't. When dealing with editors and finding them a bit *insensitive* to your plight, bear in mind that accepting your manuscript could lose them their job. That's extreme, of course. It probably won't. But it could. Editors lose their jobs for all sorts of reasons. These reasons sometimes have to do with books they bought, sometimes with ones they didn't.

Editors are painfully aware of the risk they run when returning flawed work from gifted writers. They are worried-excited that at any given moment an aspiring writer is sitting at a kitchen table in Tuscaloosa, Alabama, pounding out another *Gone with the Wind*. Editors dread the thought that this submission might get lost in their slush pile or—even worse—be discovered in some rival's. That's how tribalism works for aspiring writers. Publishing people are competitive. It's one reason they do consider submissions from writers they haven't heard of. Editors and agents can no more turn their backs on new writers than a baseball team can ignore developing rookies. Nor would they want to.

No matter how wary, weary, and wan pub people can seem, they're always on the lookout for writing from new voices that they hope will excite readers as much as it does them. Any editor lives for the experience of picking up a manuscript with an unfamiliar name on the title page and feeling her neck hairs rise as she begins to read. Editors want to get good manuscripts from new writers. They'd love to be their Henry Higgins. Editors can't make any money or have any fun by returning all submissions from unknown writers that land on their desk. Editors are no less immersed in dreams and fantasies than writers, just different dreams and fantasies. Beneath those jaded exteriors beat the yearning hearts of romantic teenagers. According to Michael Korda, manuscript reading has "a kind of Don Juan–like quality . . . the next one, or the one after, might be the love of one's life." Anthea Disney, the former head of HarperCollins, had a similar take. "It's a very emotional business," said Disney. "You're not selling Nike. You are falling in love with properties."

In their own way, editors are romantics, fantasizers, dreamers. I once heard an agent ask an editor why it was that she had an easier time selling a two-sentence book idea scribbled on a postcard than a completed manuscript. "That's easy," said the editor. "The two sentences give me a lot more opportunity to dream."

Readers

In the pre-e-mail era, correspondence from readers was forwarded to me by my publisher. *Is There Life after High School?* elicited many such letters. In this book I was a little rough on high school's "innies," the jocks, cheerleaders, and yearbook editors who sat at their own table in the cafeteria. In response, an ex-cheerleader in Texas wrote to assure me that many a woman who once led cheers had a thought or two in her head. From the other side of the cafeteria, a long, passionate letter came from a Californian who said "How dare you!" for my presumption in calling myself an outie. She then listed the criterion for being a *real* outie, like having your phone number scribbled on the wall of the boys' bathroom. My favorite response came from "Melissa," a high school junior in Illinois who told me she'd been down in the dumps because no one asked her to dance at sock hops. Reading my book had reassured Melissa that there *would* be life after high school for such as she, and that the classmates who ignored her were destined to "drown in their own blood."

It would be hard to keep writing books without occasional indications that someone actually reads them. Once a writer scribbles his message on paper, tucks it in a bottle, and throws this bottle into the sea, he has no idea if it will ever reach any shore, let alone be read. If someone does, and sends a message back—praise God!—the writer has evidence that all his work has not been in vain. That is why authors (at least those who aren't buried in fan mail, which is to say most of them) have an almost childlike gratitude for responses from those who actually *read* something they wrote, and seem to have made sense of it. Even critical letters, even those that correct errors, indicate that a correspondent has given one's book careful scrutiny. It is like that rare conversation in which one feels *heard*. Except in this case the reader cared enough to search out paper and pen, or find the writer's e-mail address, and let him know.

"All sorts of pleasant and intelligent people read the books and write thoughtful letters about them," John Cheever told an interviewer. "I don't know who they are, but they are marvelous and seem to live quite independently of the prejudices of advertising, journalism, and the cranky academic world." Cheever said that the room where he worked had a window looking out upon some woods, and he liked to think "that these earnest, lovable, and mysterious readers" were scattered among its trees.

No writer is beyond being touched, and encouraged, by reassuring messages from readers. Stephen King said he has regularly been moved by the many letters readers send him, including some that are almost religious in tone. "At times," wrote bell hooks, "when I have felt deeply discouraged, affirmative reader response has been one of the factors enabling me to continue. . . . I would not have written so many books without the passion of readers, without their urging me to write more."

Readers are indispensable to writers. A writer without a reader is just someone muttering to himself. Writing and reading constitute a silent conversation. Communing with each other through a book, readers and writers can consider matters that might be hard to discuss out loud. (If the book's any good, that's what they *ought* to be doing.) In the process, an intimacy can emerge like that enjoyed by any two people who share secrets. *Friendship* is a term often used by writers to characterize their relationship with readers. Proust considered this friendship of the purest grade because it wasn't based on hypocrisy, social convention, or the desire to ingratiate. "With books," wrote Proust, "no amiability. These friends, if we spend an evening with them, it is truly because we desire them. In their case, at least, we leave often only with regret. And when we have left them, with none of those thoughts which spoil friendship: What did they think of us?—Didn't we lack tact?—Did we please? . . . All these agitations of friendship expire at the threshold of that pure and calm friendship that is reading. Nor is there any deference: we laugh at what Molière says only to the exact degree we find him funny; when he bores us, and when we have decidedly had enough of being with him, we put him back in his place as bluntly as if he had neither genius nor fame."

Now that e-mailing has become a way of life, like most computerized writers I find that my contact with readers is up, my sense of isolation down, and I'm happy for it. One great virtue of information technology is that it facilitates reader-writer interaction. The many readers of *The Courage to Write* who took the time to e-mail encouraged me to think about writing a second book on writing. This is the result.

Keeping Hope Alive

*The great secret of writing is not becoming a writer, it's
staying a writer.*

Harlan Ellison

Australian writer Janette Turner Hospital developed what she
called an "emergency drill for bad times." In addition to compiling fatuous rejections, scathing reviews, and other humiliations
suffered by noted writers, Hospital's drill included taking time to
console herself, trusting her instincts, and remaining defiant.
When all else failed, Hospital proposed this strategy for dealing
with multiple rejections or rotten reviews: "Have one stiff drink,
say five Hail Mary's, and ten Fuck-You's, and get back to work."

Keeping morale up over the course of a project, or career,
is a daunting task. Many writers can't, and fall by the wayside.
Something that distinguishes working writers from terminally
discouraged ones is that the former stay at their desk. Those
who persist don't do so blindly. They develop coping strategies,
ways to keep hope alive. Here are ten of them.

1) Create a Consolation File

During seven years of repeated rejections at the outset of his
career, Frederick Busch kept close at hand a list of every pub-

lisher that had turned down Malcolm Lowry's *Under the Volcano*. As the list of publishers who returned his own work grew, Busch sought solace by reviewing Lowry's. That list—the one Lowry's agent sent him after concluding that *Under the Volcano* was unpublishable—included:

Farrar & Rinehart
Harcourt, Brace
Houghton Mifflin
Alfred Knopf
J. P. Lippincott
Little, Brown
Random House
Scribner's
Simon & Schuster
Duell, Sloan & Pearce
Dial Press
Story Press

Like Busch and Hospital, many writers make a hobby out of compiling information about famous writers who suffered repeated rejection. One called his compilation a *hairshirt* file. On bleak days when all seemed for naught, he opened that folder and reviewed its contents. This tactic is surprisingly common among working writers. They read a lot about published writers who were once unpublished writers, looking for consolation more than for guidance. When a longtime editor named William Targ (the same William Targ who paid Mario Puzo $5,000 for *The Godfather*) couldn't persuade anyone to publish his own novel, he kept reminding himself that forty-two publishers rejected Samuel Beckett's *Murphy* before a British editor bought it for twenty-five pounds—about $100. Like

Beckett, Targ eventually found a publisher, several in fact, in various countries.

I, too, have a file with information like this. Its contents remind me that when Gail Godwin's agent was unable to sell her first novel (*The Perfectionists*), she refused to represent her any longer; that Thackeray had to pay to have *Vanity Fair* published; and that a *San Francisco Examiner* editor returned an article to Rudyard Kipling with a note saying, "This isn't a kindergarten for amateur writers. I'm sorry, Mr. Kipling, but you just don't know how to use the English language."

Reading about the frustrations of other writers makes me feel less alone with my own. Writers read about each other a lot, searching for morsels of reassurance. They study how discouraged famous writers once were. They note how many times immortal writers had their work rejected. They even find solace in the eccentric writing techniques employed by many. Essayist Fran Lebowitz once said that if she could meet Proust, the first thing she'd ask him would be, "So how many hours a day do you write? Do you write at night, or when?" Why are writers so fascinated by the minutiae of each others' working habits? It could simply be a way of trying to answer one of life's persistent questions: "Are other writers as addled as I am?"

Reading not just about the rejections but the frustration, anxiety, despair of famous writers is most encouraging. The best texts are ones that weren't meant for publication, ones in which working authors feel free to reveal things they wouldn't want Oprah to know: Woolf's diary, Cheever's journals, Fitzgerald's letters, and those of Flaubert. Note how frustrated Flaubert felt while writing *Madame Bovary*, how jealous Cheever was of other writers, and how desperate Virginia Woolf often felt, even at the peak of her writing prowess, and long before her 1941 suicide. "My mind turned by anxiety, or other cause, from its scrutiny of blank paper, is like a lost child," she wrote in 1919, "—wandering the house, sitting on the bottom step to cry." Earlier that year Woolf fretted about her hunger for praise: "Unpraised I find it hard to start writing in the morning; but the dejection lasts only 30 minutes, and once I start I forget all about it."

2) Study Acknowledgments

Most readers skip the acknowledgments page in books. Writers analyze them. Acknowledgments can be a treasure chest of useful and reassuring information. Here is where, explicitly or implicitly, writers are most likely to admit suffering from AFD syndrome and suggest how they got beyond it. They so routinely acknowledge those who *encouraged* them, who *supported* them, who kept their *spirits up*, that—whether they say so or not—you know these authors had to have been discouraged, and in desperate need of support from those whom they are now acknowledging.

I've just finished reading a delightful memoir called *The Prize Winner of Defiance, Ohio.* The confident writing style of its first-time author, Terry Ryan, made her text read as though it just flowed from her pen. But in her acknowledgments at the end, in addition to relatives, friends, and teachers from high school, Ryan thanked her agent for unusually energetic help, a colleague for "unflagging enthusiasm and hard work on my behalf," a manuscript consultant who helped her "in more ways than one," an Internet columnist "who was there when the first word struck the page and pushed me to write the second," and a friend of her mother's who "patiently reviewed my drafts and offered support of a kind I could get nowhere else. When I told her I was working alone on this project, she said, 'No, you aren't. You've got me.'" Ryan then proceeded to list the names of thirty-one people, as well as members of the Northglenn #1 Study Group of Lakewood, Colorado, "for readings of various versions of the manuscript and ongoing encouragement."

In virtually any book's acknowledgments, *encouragement* is second only to *thanks* among words authors use to acknowledge those who helped them. To cite just a few:

> I am indebted to all my friends, family, and teachers who have offered me their encouragement.
>
> JOANNA TORREY, *Hungry*

> I am particularly indebted to Miriam Gross for her encouragement.
>
> ALAIN DE BOTTON, *How Proust Can Change Your Life*

> [a long list of names] provided encouragement and help.
>
> PAUL EDDY, *Flint*

> I would like to thank a number of others who in one way or another encouraged me.
>
> CAROL SHIELDS, *Unless*

Studying acknowledgments confirms three things: (1) these authors felt discouraged while writing their book; (2) they sought, and received, support from encouragers; and (3) their spirits revived enough for them to complete their book and get it published.

3) Attend Courses and Conferences

Even though Proust once said that an hour spent talking was an hour of writing time gone forever, he himself was a great conversationalist and boulevardier. So were Beckett and Wilde.

Take a tip from such authors. In the absence of literary cafés, contemporary writers-in-progress enroll in courses and attend conferences—partly to learn their craft, but even more to put themselves in settings where they're likely to find encouragers. That alone is worth the price of admission. As one participant in the Antioch Writers' Workshop later wrote its director, "I thought I would get my face smashed because I have been avoiding committing to my writing. What I got was love, support, encouragement, valuable criticism, suggestions, and friendships."

A good writing course or conference will feature information, feedback, and reassurance. Supportive teachers and classmates can be found in such settings. Some of the best ones are not necessarily well known. Outstanding teachers often toil in obscure institutions or adult education programs whose faculty care more about their students than their status. These gatherings can also be ones in which participants feel safe to share invaluable information with each other, such as "your lead got my attention," or, "I found it hard to pay attention toward the end." And: "I think you're going to make it."

Writing courses and conferences—the right ones—are citadels of encouragement. (The wrong ones, including some that feature all-star writers, almost gleefully try to deconstruct their students.) Such gatherings consider it part of their mission to offer hope. Unlike members of other professions, writers have few natural opportunities to network. They must seek them out and sometimes pay for the privilege. This is one among many reasons that attending the occasional writers' gathering can be a good investment. Courses and conferences offer an opportunity to mingle and connect as much as to learn about writing. Here one is likely to meet colleagues, teachers, even possible mentors. At gatherings that include editors and agents, aspiring writers make direct contact with those who are in a position to help them get published. At the very least, they provide an in-the-flesh opportunity to see what pub people look like, get a sense of how they perceive the world, and a feeling for how best to approach them. Authors who were "discovered" at writing conferences include Fannie Flagg, Robert Ferrigno, and Isabel Allende, who prepared herself to write novels by attending the Squaw Valley Community of Writers. That's where Amy Tan also found the mentor who invited her to join an ongoing writers' group she led, and later introduced Tan to the woman who became Tan's agent. Jean Auel found her agent at the Willamette Writers Writing Conference.

4) Group

Former U.S. senator and presidential aspirant Fred Harris has enjoyed a second career as a novelist. You'd think that being a successful politician would instill enough self-confidence to make encouragement unnecessary in this new vocation. Hardly. Rather than rely on his laurels and contacts, the Albuquerque retiree approached this intimidating task in a practical-minded way: by reading books on how to get published, querying agents (most of whom felt his Oklahoma-based historical mystery wouldn't sell, until one in Dallas took him on), and attending writers' conferences. Finally, Harris joined the First Friday Group—a monthly gathering of Albuquerque writers that included Tony Hillerman.

The enthusiasm kindled by courses and conferences can fade fast once participants return to their lonely desk. That's where ongoing groups such as First Friday come in handy. Writing groups may or may not help members become better writers, but they are a capital source of camaraderie and support. This is not to be sneezed at. More than one New York writer has attributed the completion of a manuscript to being able to work in the Writers Room, a converted loft in lower Manhattan that combines elements of a workplace and informal support group.

Some argue that writing is a solitary business whose frustration can only be endured, not alleviated. Why? Writers need support no less than any other creative person, perhaps more so. Groups can offer that support. At the very least, a good group can relieve the loneliness, frustration, and despair that goes with the writer's territory. Long after they became household names, authors such as Maxine Kumin, Mary Higgins Clark, Jean Auel, Anne Sexton, Ezra Pound, and many others continued to meet with groups of colleagues. At that stage of their career they benefited less from critiquing of their work than from the simple solace of being among peers. Writers feel relief in each other's company. What seems strange to civilians makes perfect sense to colleagues. *"Oh, you write in bed? So do I. Do you get dressed first? I use a Waterman fountain pen. What do you use? How do you deal with relatives who think you've written about them and don't like it? Or the ones you don't write about who feel snubbed?"*

Providing company for isolated peers is the baseline rationale for writing groups. But these gatherings serve many purposes other than fellowship. Good ones motivate, inspire, and goad members to write. Going in, they impose a deadline. Coming out, they send members home invigorated. More than once, I've left a writers' group meeting in which the response of colleagues to my work was so helpful that I attacked a manuscript with renewed enthusiasm—sometimes that very night.

Years after one group I belonged to held its final meeting, fellow member Richard Peacock sent me galleys of his first book, which was about to be published by Warner. Peacock said he doubted that he could have written this book without our help. By this he didn't mean help with his grammar, style, or structure. The most valuable thing our group gave him, said Peacock, was simply the *idea* that he could write a book.

5) Bone Up

Flaubert liked to wax eloquent about the integrity of the artist. The author also once upbraided a colleague for not befriending every man at the Comédie Française, for which he wanted to write, and sleeping with every woman there.

Most of us aren't in a position to pull that one off. But we can become better acquainted with the whys and wherefores of publishing by doing our homework. This means going to hear published writers speak, especially those who will discuss the process of writing and submission as much as the product. It means reading not just books about writing and writers but those about publishing, including memoirs of editors and agents. Browsing *Publishers Weekly* and publisherslunch.com can be helpful. Publications such as *The Writer, Writer's Digest,* and *Writer's Market* have their value, and were invaluable to writers such as Eudora Welty, Margaret Atwood, Mary Higgins Clark, and Stephen King in their apprentice phase. Far more noted writers than care to admit it studied back issues of *Writer's Digest* and devoured books like *The Insider's Guide to Getting Published* before anyone took note of their writing.

The information explosion makes it possible for contemporary writers to educate themselves in ways that were difficult even a few years ago. A treasure trove of information about submission etiquette, editorial guidelines, and the culture of publishing can be found on the Internet. Doing this homework helps writers see things from the perspective of the publishing tribe. That's why I devour whatever I can get my hands on about pub people. In doing this, I'm less interested in "101

Ways to Romance an Editor" than in familiarizing myself with their take on the world so we can communicate better. Reading about pub people and their ways makes me feel as though I'm not plunging blind into a foreign culture, that I know something about the natives and their customs. It also gives me tangible information. Those of us who didn't attend writing programs in college need to develop alternatives to the old boy and girl network enjoyed by those who did. Reading broadly is one way to do this, including—again—acknowledgments.

It's a rare author who doesn't acknowledge his or her agent and editor. Here is an important payoff for studying this page in books. Shrewd writers keep track of editors and agents who have worked with a book similar to the one they want to write. When contacting someone on their list, they mention that fact. This is bound to impress that person favorably. They will note that this correspondent has taken the initiative to ferret them out. Few writers do.

6) Be Professional

Agents and editors are swamped with submissions from dilettantes. This is good news for those who approach them knowledgeably. The more professional you are when contacting an agency or publisher, the more seriously your submission will be taken.

Established agents typically get 100 or more submissions a week. That sounds discouraging. But here's the good news: The vast majority of these submissions are not worth a second look. Some are obviously part of a mass mailing. Others are completely inappropriate for the agent in question. Still more are filled with errors, are sloppy in form, or are accompanied by an inappropriate letter (cute, chatty, chummy, etc.). If you're doing your job, you are not competing with everyone else who's contacted that agent; only the small minority who do so professionally.

This calls for doing more homework. An agent or editor can tell pretty quickly if you are among the handful who do. The bane of agents and editors is fledgling writers who make little effort to find out who they are and what interests them before making contact. In the Google era there is no excuse for being anything less than well informed about pub people whom you approach. If you can't do so much as a Web search about an agent or editor before contacting that individual, what does this say about your seriousness?

Those who do make that type of effort present an impressive calling card. Noting early in a query letter that you're familiar with books an agent has represented or ones an editor has edited tells that person right off the bat that this is not part of a mass mailing (or, if it is, it's a remarkably clever one). "I am always impressed when someone has taken the trouble to find out that I represent a writer they admire," observed agent Stuart Krichevsky, "and whose work has some kind of affinity with theirs. It takes you right out of the pile of letters and e-mails that come flooding in daily that have clearly been sent to every agent in the known universe (sometimes we even get e-mails that show hundreds of addresses in the header!) and helps us recognize you as a professional. That's really what you're asking—to be taken seriously—and the best way to do that is to show that you know who we are, and take our work seriously."

The same thing is true of editors. While it is true that most major publishers say they will no longer consider submissions that don't come from an agent, of course they will if an author approaches them appropriately and they like the author's pitch. Even though an unsolicited manuscript will at best get a cursory glance from an overworked intern, a brief, well-composed letter of inquiry will catch the eye of nearly any editor. When she did not want to make changes to her manuscript that were suggested by agents, Frances Sherwood wrote directly to the editor in chief of Farrar, Straus & Giroux. This editor found the first-time novelist's letter so compelling that he asked to see her manuscript for *Vindication*, then published it to good reviews and Book-of-the-Month Club selection.

7) Go Easy on Yourself

Going easy on yourself means not returning to your desk immediately after receiving a demoralizing rejection. Not setting your standards so high that you can't reach them. Not duking it out with your inner censors on each and every occasion. "When your Daemon is in charge," said Kipling, "do not try to think consciously. Drift, wait, and obey."

Take a 12-step approach. Don't look too far down the road. Don't look farther than tomorrow or even sundown. Accumulate writing as you accumulate savings: gradually. "Abandon the idea that you are ever going to finish," suggested Steinbeck. "Lose track of the 400 pages and write just one page for each day; it helps. Then when it gets finished, you are always surprised."

Don't worry too much about your frame of mind. Write on good days and bad. Later do a blind taste test and see if you can tell what pages were written on which days. Few writers can.

Realizing this makes experienced authors pragmatic. That attitude, in turn, keeps them recording words on paper. The stalled writer—no matter how talented—is typically one who's vowed, "If I can't make my words on paper look every bit as good as the ones I set out to write, I just won't write them!" This is a recipe for writer's block. Veteran writers know it's an impossible dream and have stopped trying. They understand that the only real cure for writer's block is to lower their standards. That may sound cynical, and defeatist, but it's actually what all writers do (those who are still writing, anyway). Unlike dropouts, working writers come to terms with the fact that they'll never write the work they intended to write. "The poem in the head is always perfect," said Stanley Kunitz. "Resistance starts when you try to convert it into language." Yet the output of lowered-standards writers such as Kunitz can far exceed any that could possibly be achieved by a writer mired in perfectionism. Successful perfectionists cannot be writers; only failed perfectionists. David Foster Wallace compared his flawed novels to a damaged, repulsive offspring that he loved nonetheless. "The fiction always comes out so horrifically defective," wrote Wallace, "so hideous a betrayal of all your hopes for it—a cruel and repellent caricature of the perfection of its conception— yes, understand: grotesque because *imperfect*."

Actual writers like Wallace know this will always be true, that they'll never write the book they meant to write, but continue to write anyway. They take the philosophical approach of Ovid, who said about one of his works, "Whatever faults may be found in this unpolished poem, the author would have corrected had time allowed."

8) Be Tactical

When Fran Lebowitz visited Sotheby's one afternoon, an employee showed her a manuscript by Mark Twain that it planned to auction. What the staff at Sotheby's couldn't figure out was why the author had scribbled numbers in the margins every few pages. They were about to ask a Twain scholar. Don't bother, said Lebowitz. She'd tell them. Twain was counting how many words he'd written. The Sotheby's man thought that was absurd. No it wasn't, said Lebowitz. To prove her point, she challenged him to count the manuscript's words and compare them with the scribbled numbers. These two figures matched. The man from Sotheby's wondered if this meant that Twain was being paid by the word. "It may have nothing to do with being paid by the word," Lebowitz suggested. "Twain might have told himself he had to write this many words a day, and he would wonder, Am I there yet? Like a little kid in the back of a car. Are we there yet?"

How did Lebowitz know this? Because she counted words too. Many writers do. Ernest Hemingway recorded his day's output on the side of a cardboard box: 450, 575, 1,250, et cetera. Anthony Burgess strived for 1,000 publishable words a day. So did Irwin Shaw and Joseph Wambaugh. Evelyn Waugh and the young Norman Mailer went for 2,000, as did James Thurber and P. G. Wodehouse.

Word counters may be extreme, but their systematic approach to writing is more the norm than the exception among professional writers. They know that resisting the temptation to leave their desk is the hardest part of their job. This is why authors come up with so many strategies to keep themselves writing, no matter how absurd these might seem to civilians. Early in his career, Erskine Caldwell found it easier to write if he stayed in motion. Caldwell rode buses all over the country, debarking now and again to scribble words on paper. Then the novelist began taking night boats between Boston and New York—the Fall River Line, the New Bedford Line, the Cape Cod Line. "The rhythm of the water might have helped my sentence structure a little," Caldwell later reflected, "at least I thought it did." Kent Haruf wrote *Plainsong* in the unheated basement of his Murphysboro, Illinois, home with a watch cap pulled over his eyes. This kept him from becoming too analytical, Haruf thought, helped him "get in touch with the intuitive, the visual, the spontaneous, without any attention to detail and syntax. It takes away the terror when you're blind and you can't go back and rewrite a sentence."

Writers are very tactical people. They must be—to outwit the grinch of despair. Dapper Tom Wolfe sometimes wore a turtleneck and khakis while writing, in part because he would have been embarrassed to leave the house dressed that way. For similar reasons, Oscar Wilde worked in a white dressing gown modeled after the one Balzac wore at his desk. Alice Munro, Beryl Bainbridge, and countless others wrote in their nightclothes. Martha Grimes wrote in bed with fountain pens, using fourteen different shades of ink to keep from getting bored. Sometimes Grimes changed ink color midmanuscript to trick herself into imagining a new hue would produce fresher writing.

Few writers work in great spaces. Some deliberately eschew them. Like trapeze artists and pizza chefs, many end up working in public. James Redfield wrote *The Celestine Prophecy* in a Waffle House near Birmingham, Alabama. Doing so helped him focus on those readers he was trying to reach, said Redfield: everyday people with ordinary problems and spiritual hungers. Jay Parini found a similar benefit from writing books in his booth at Lou's Diner. "What I liked about Lou's was the distant clatter of dishes," said Parini, "the purr of conversation, and the occasional interruption of a friend. Restaurants provide a kind of white noise, but—unlike real white noise—the sound is human. Noses are blown. People cough. You're reminded of the world of phlegm and digestion. And you feel connected."

9) Indulge Dubious Motives

After he was awarded the Nobel Prize for literature, Saul Bellow had to pinch himself. As the younger sibling of two wealthy businessmen, he told a friend, "All I started out to do was show up my brothers."

One of the more challenging aspects of being a writer is having to acknowledge one's less-than-stellar motives. Ego. Anger. Envy. Spitefulness. Getting even. Showing off. To name just a few.

Over the course of her distinguished career, Margaret Atwood made a hobby of collecting reasons for writing that authors mention in their autobiographies, during press interviews, on talk shows, and during "conversations in the backs of bookstores before the dreaded group signing." From the long list Atwood recorded in *Negotiating with the Dead*, my personal favorites include:

> To make money so I could sneer at those who
>   formerly sneered at me.
> To show the bastards.
> To act out antisocial behavior for which I would have
>   been punished in real life.
> Because I hated the idea of having a job.
> To justify my failures in school.
> To rectify the imperfections of my miserable
>   childhood.
> To make myself appear more interesting than I
>   actually was.
> To cope with my depression.
> Because I was possessed.
> To thumb my nose at death.

Not a pretty picture. So? It's writers' words that interest readers, not their reasons for recording them.

Putting up with solitude, frustration, and the irresistible urge to watch *As the World Turns* calls for mining whatever energy sources are at hand. In chapter 3 we considered the determination to *show* discourager-goads through the success of one's writing. This is a surprisingly common motive among writers candid enough to admit it. Mary Gaitskill is one. Gaitskill conceded that this motivation is "embarrassing, it's base, and it smells bad, but it's also an angry little engine that could."

Writer after writer has paid tribute to anger as a superb source of energy. You might be surprised to discover how many apparently mild-mannered writers harbor furious demons, how many literary Clark Kents step into phone booths before writing so they can change into—Dr. Evil. When an interviewer asked Philip Roth if he had a "Roth reader" in mind while writing, the author replied that actually he was more likely to have an "anti-Roth" reader in mind. "I think, 'How he is going to hate this!' That can be just the encouragement I need."

Like patients in therapy, writers often stumble on hidden lodes of rage within themselves as they write (leading many to stop writing). This can be a scary experience. At the same time, that anger can be converted into a bubbling geyser of drive, focus, and motivation. "I like to write when I feel spiteful," said D. H. Lawrence; "it's like having a good sneeze."

The angriest contemporary writer of all—the troubadour of rage, if you will—was William Gass. In order to produce his best work, said the novelist, he *had* to be mad. Not that this was hard for him; Gass was angry most of the time. But on days when his anger ebbed, so did his output. That made him mad. Then the words started to flow again. Fury was always the flywheel.

An inability to accept their mixed motives has driven many gifted writers from the field. (*What sort of person do you think I am?*) Those who stick around not only come to terms with their dubious reasons for writing, but make good use of them. Gertrude Stein said she wrote for praise, William Faulkner for glory, James Salter "to be admired." Many authors, including John Grisham and Sue Grafton, have said they use their writing as a tool of retribution against those who wronged them. John Hawkes went so far as to call any work of fiction an act of revenge.

"There is no wrong motive for writing fiction," concluded John Gardner. "No motive is too low for art; finally it's the art, not the motive, that we judge."

10) Get Busy on Your Own Behalf

Aspiring writers generally see getting published as the answer to their prayers. Veteran authors know that this is when their problems begin. The unfortunate truth is that once publishers put a book in the marketplace, they don't necessarily back it.

In an early draft I called this section "Suppose They Published a Book and No One Noticed?" It happens. Far more books are ignored than promoted by their own publishers. Among major trade publishers especially, abandonment is the rule, not the exception. Authors of neglected books then have a choice. They can retire to a corner, pick their hangnails, and whimper about lack of support from their publisher. Or they can get busy on their own behalf. They can *force* their publisher to support their book. Anita Diamant did just that. As unsold copies of Diamant's novel *The Red Tent* were about to be shredded, the author came up with the names of 1,000 rabbis she thought might be interested in her biblical epic. Many were, and told others. *The Red Tent* went on to become a major bestseller, with more than a million copies in print.

If you are lucky enough to get your books published, and I hope you are, but unlucky enough to have your book be neglected, take a tip from Diamant. Approaching staff members at your publisher on a "What can *I* do?" basis is far more productive than blasting them for their indolence. Develop your own marketing strategy. Contact reporters whose interests dovetail with the subject matter of your book. Request more comp copies to mail out and generate buzz (ask if your publisher will at least pay postage). Create a Web site. Search for other Web sites that attract those who might be interested in a book like yours. Arrange your own signings. Do a regional tour, driving yourself and staying with friends or at the Motel 6. Most publishers are practical-minded. If you present them with a proposal for a substantial amount of publicity at a bargain, they will pay attention. Pub people know better than anyone that such efforts can pay off.

When John Grisham's first novel, *A Time to Kill*, was stalled in the marketplace, he bought 1,000 of the 5,000 copies printed and—accompanied by his friend Bobby Moak—sold them from the trunk of his Volvo at book signings he arranged himself: at libraries, reading group meetings, and small bookstores in Mississippi and Arkansas. (One trunkload got rained on and became landfill.) Outside a mall bookstore the fledgling author sat in excruciating solitude at a table where everyone could see how little business he was doing. Customers shunned Grisham as they might a homeless man. An old friend from law school walked by and stopped to chat for half an hour but didn't buy a book. "It was hell getting rid of those dadgum things," Moak later recalled. "Hell!" On the other hand, copies of that first printing of Grisham's first novel that were so hard to sell are now worth a small fortune. With a kick-start from the author's energetic efforts on his own behalf, *A Time to Kill* eventually got a toehold in the marketplace, building a foundation for Grisham's later success. In subsequent printings this novel sold over 9 million copies.

Grisham is legendary in the industry as the most successful of the "trunk authors" (those who initially sold books out of their own car's trunk). Terry McMillan is another one. When

McMillan's publisher ignored her first novel, *Mama*, the single mother of a five-year-old boy decided to do her own personal trunk show. Capitalizing on suggestions she read in Judith Appelbaum's *How to Get Happily Published*, McMillan toured the country in her car, touting her book to booksellers and others whom she'd spent weeks writing. The African-American author was faced not only with the skepticism confronting any first-time author but the added conviction of publishers and booksellers that there was no market for mainstream fiction by black novelists. McMillan proved them wrong. She didn't just find an audience—she *created* one. Many of her customers hadn't been readers of novels until they started reading *Mama*, then *Waiting to Exhale*, and *How Stella Got Her Groove Back*. McMillan forced publishers to face the fact that the audience of black readers they thought didn't exist was simply one they didn't know how to reach. She taught them that newspaper reviews and TV talk show appearances were not the best way to contact members of this reading community. Radio chat, book circles, and word of mouth were.

Nonauthors, especially ones with decent salaries or dependable trust funds, sometimes wonder if authors like McMillan aren't a tad too "self-promotional." I always want to ask these skeptics, "What's your point?" Twain, Whitman, and Hemingway were diligent self-promoters. So was Lillian Hellman, and George Orwell, in his discreet British manner. Imagine what use history's literary self-promoters could have made of today's on-line resources. Web sites galore for Twain. Pop-up ads for Whitman. Streaming video of Hemingway boxing. Lillian Hellman sharing her wartime exploits with iVillagers. George Orwell discussing *Animal Farm* on Salon.com.

In the best of all possible worlds, one's book would shoot so far above the other tens of thousands of books published every year that authors would have no need to toot their own literary horns. Should this not happen, as it probably won't, and authors don't take an active role in calling attention to their work—who will?

Successful authors routinely spend far more time touting their books than they ever dreamed would be necessary. Such stories speak to two traits these authors share: faith in themselves and willingness to work on their own behalf. They whine and feel sorry for themselves, sure. Who wouldn't? But they don't stop with whining and self-pity. They become their own publicist, sales rep, and chauffeur. These are determined people, determined to show every dubious publisher, nonreviewer, and skeptical teacher from high school that there is an audience for their writing, a market for their wares.

You could say that peddling your own wares is beneath you. Or that it's your publisher's job, not yours. And you'd be right. You'd also be a writer on the path to obscurity. Your book is your child. Any parent will do almost anything for his or her child. So should any author. You are the only person in the world who is 100 percent committed to your book. Act like it. Get busy on its behalf. Reach out to readers. It is your good fortune to be writing in a time when there are more ways than ever for those who write to communicate with those who read.

· 10 ·

The Best of Times

The invention of movable type created opportunities for
writers that could barely be imagined in Gutenberg's day.
The opportunities that await writers in the near future
are immeasurably greater.

Jason Epstein, editor

When it comes to the book business, much gloom and doom
can be heard. Publishers consolidate; chain stores kill off independents; blockbusters prevail; reading gives way to Net surfing; the book may be dying. Things look bad. Or so we're
told. There's a flip side, however, a bright side that doesn't
receive comparable attention. As far as writers are concerned,
one might even say that bad news is the B side, good news the
A side.

James Atlas, an editor and literary biographer with a particular interest in postwar authors, has concluded that it's easier
to get published today than it was half a century ago. More
help than ever is available to writers: in books, magazines, Web
sites, classes, conferences, and groups. As a result, agents and
editors note the rising proportion of well-informed writers who
contact them. According to the study that found 81 percent of
Americans would like to write a book, 6 million actually have.
Walker & Company president George Gibson sees hope for
publishers like himself in the unprecedented number of people

who are writing today. "The act of writing," said Gibson, "as it has always been, is an act of faith, and if the numbers of the faithful are growing, the intellectual health of publishing is ultimately in good hands. Internal pressures may have forced publishers to think in short-term, mass-market terms; external factors insist they keep a broader view."

This is just one among many reasons that there has never been a better time to write. That may sound preposterous to discouraged writers, but it's true. Although the number of books published per year is usually given as 50,000, more than twice that many ISBN numbers are assigned annually, suggesting that far more books than ever are being published by all manner of publishers. For writers, this means that more vehicles are available for them to convey their words to receptive eyes: presses big and small, e-publishers, and through their own efforts. An explosion of book clubs and readers' groups has put books in hands that once only held remote control devices. These groups have helped accomplish the best thing that could possibly happen for reading, as far as authors are concerned: they've made it *fashionable*. A revealing—and reassuring—1999 Gallup Poll found that 84 percent of respondents said they'd read a book all the way through in the preceding year. Thirty-six years earlier, less than half of those polled made that claim. A decade before that, in 1952, only 18 percent said they'd read a book within the past year.

Despite all the dire predictions about their demise, Americans spend more money than ever on books. An increasing number of merchants now sell them: not just Books-a-Million, Borders, and Barnes & Noble but Price Clubs, Target, Wal-Mart, JC Penney, Kroger's, and countless niche stores that carry titles related to their specialty (to say nothing of the many Web sites that sell books to readers who would rather not leave their keyboard). It may be true that the rise of megabookstores and on-line booksellers has put too much emphasis on bestsellers. But their rise is not all bad for writers at every level. Big chain stores have helped increase the volume of books being sold overall. They host lots of signings—a commonplace today, a rarity not that long ago—and offer rooms where reading and writing groups can meet. Chains provide bookstores where none existed before, and a more inviting environment for customers who feel uncomfortable in smaller, more literary bookshops. A wider range of books can be found on chain store shelves than the average independent store has room to stock. And Amazon.com strives to sell nearly any book available, in or out of print.

On the other side of the fence, independent bookstores are rallying, with salutary results for writers. Their rapid decline in the face of competition from the chains has arrested. Those that survived—and new ones that have started—are better equipped to compete with chains. As ever, their strength is in their personal relationship with book buyers. Independent booksellers do more "handselling," recommending specific titles to customers. Titles recommended by Book Sense, the independents' influential consortium, come from a broader pool than those anointed by chain stores. Few of these books are urban or trendy. Some are offbeat. In this way, Book Sense has encouraged receptivity to a wider range of titles by publishers.

Big and small, bookstores will never die. Amazon.com does not and cannot replace the opportunity to browse, caress books, sip a cappuccino, attend a signing, meet the love of one's life. So long as human beings have an urge to mingle with kindred spirits, there will always be bookstores. That urge also underlies the renaissance of reading groups, among older readers in particular. The maturing of America may be bad news for health clubs, but it's good news for authors, publishers, and booksellers. Those over fifty-five buy a disproportionate number of books. As baby boomers age, they're no less likely than their parents and grandparents to read—the difference being that there are so many more boomers, reading more books than ever. True, their children and grandchildren may not read as much as earlier generations did. But that doesn't mean they don't read at all. My own two boys, who spend an inordinate amount of time before a computer screen, like to take a break with a book. Both reach a point where they're sated with electronic input, where their eyes need to rest on something as tangible as print on paper with its absence of flicker, and their aching wrists need a break from keyboard tapping and mouse movement. My sons are not alone. Even tech types tend to print out on-line text of any length before reading it. (I'm told this is true of Microsoft's Bill Gates.) There seems to be a limit to how many pixelized words our eyes can accommodate.

Technology has an upside for authors, of course; many upsides. The job of start-up publishers has been made easier by software programs that facilitate desktop publishing, book design, fulfillment, and billing. Computers also make it easier than ever for authors to publish their own work. In the not-too-distant future, on-demand printing presses that produce one book at a time will make it viable to publish writing with even a few prospective readers. Currently, there are more magazines, newsletters, small publishers, Web sites, and e-publishers than ever to convey writers' words to readers. On-line publishing is an encouraging work in progress. There are unimagined ways to deliver writing to readers of the future. These are all very positive developments, unusually good news for writers.

Chicken Soup for Small-Press Dummies

During George W. Bush's second year in office, every major trade house in New York rejected a proposed biography of Laura Bush because they didn't think enough readers would be interested in the first lady. Adams Media in Avon, Massachusetts, saw things differently. When Adams published Laura Bush's biography, it became an instant bestseller with hundreds of thousands of copies in the marketplace.

This is a recurring pattern. Because no major publishers showed any interest in *Night*, Elie Wiesel's agent sold his autobiographical novel to start-up Hill & Wang for an advance of $250. Tom Clancy's *The Hunt for Red October* was considered so unpromising by so many major trade publishers that the author let the Naval Institute Press have it for $5,000. Naval Institute subsequently brought out Stephen Coonts's *Flight of the Intruder*, the novel that launched Coonts's career as a bestselling novelist.

Many authors who went on to become household names—including Henry Miller, Anaïs Nin, and Ernest Hemingway—were first published by small presses. Samuel Beckett's *Murphy* only appeared in the United States when upstart Grove Press took a chance on Beckett's obscure first novel, after it had been available abroad for two decades. Grove also published Gilbert Sorrentino's best-known book, *Mulligan Stew*, after twenty-eight other publishers had turned it down.

The consolidation of publishers into a few megaliths has created both problems and opportunities for writers. Problems, because there are fewer and fewer big trade houses to solicit. Opportunities, because so many small publishers have filled voids left by contracting and comatose old-line publishers. Small publishers are like new growth bursting through the loam of decayed trees in an old forest. As old trees, such as Lippin-cott, Bobbs Merrill, and Duell Sloan, mature and die, new ones sprout in the compost they leave behind. After all, every big publisher was once a small publisher. Today's Adams, Chron-icle, Sourcebooks, Workman, Newmarket, and Overlook may be tomorrow's Knopf, Crown, Doubleday, or Warner. The only difference is that there are so many more small publishers than ever. The proportion of all published books that come from small presses is growing, the proportion that come from large houses is shrinking. By the end of the twentieth century, most books in print came from small presses, in part because these publishers tend to keep their books alive far longer than larger publishers do. Nominations for awards such as the National Book Award increasingly include small-press titles. As major publishers continue to enjoy success selling books like the ones they've always sold, innovative breakthroughs come from newer, smaller houses.

The fact that new publishing ventures are founded all over the country is good news for writers. Those not headquartered in New York—most of them—are receptive to ideas that may not suit a Manhattan state of mind. *Life's Little Instruction Book* was published by Rutledge Hill Press of Nashville, Tennessee, *The Prayer of Jabez* by Multnomah in Sisters, Oregon, *How to Behave So Your Children Will, Too* by Greentree Press in Tempe, Arizona, *Conversations with God* by Hampton Roads Publishing in Charlottesville, Virginia. After so many publishers in New York told him that *Chicken Soup for the Soul* was a nonstarter, agent Jeff Herman—who lives and works in Stockbridge, Massachusetts—sold this manuscript to Health Communica-tions in Deerfield Beach, Florida.

Let's not kid ourselves. Given our druthers, most of us would rather be published by a well-known trade publisher. This is an eloquent form of validation. Now we're *real* writers,

writers worth money to a publisher we've heard of, one whose name might excite gasps of recognition at our twenty-fifth class reunion. ("You mean *Henry Holt* published your book?!") But that's not necessarily going to happen. And if it doesn't, this isn't necessarily a reflection on our work. Our ideas, our writing style (to say nothing of our ability to converse with Oprah) may not be this year's flavor or fit this decade's categories. The editor who rejected our submission may have been suffering from heartburn. Then we may have to publish with presses we—let alone our classmates—have never heard of. But this isn't necessarily the comedown one might imagine, or any comedown at all.

True, it is rare for a small press to offer a big advance. These publishers don't enjoy the marketing muscle and massive distribution channels enjoyed by larger houses. But: they are more likely to pay attention to each title on their smaller lists and keep them in print longer. In lieu of big advances, small houses tend to be more solicitous of their authors. (San Francisco's MacAdam/Cage actually *sends* its editors to meet with their authors.) Just as network television depends on cable channels for breakthroughs, big publishers use small ones as a farm system to discover new authors, entertain fresh ideas, and develop innovative ways to publish books. Flying in the face of conventional publishing wisdom that book titles should never, *ever* twit the reader, it was IDG Books in Foster City, California, that began the *Dummies* series. Outside Chicago, Sourcebooks is at the forefront of multimedia books such as the wildly successful *And the Crowd Goes Wild*.

Major publishers have repeatedly had to pay smaller publishers for rights to a book they'd originally turned down. MacAdam/Cage, for example, sold reprint rights to Anne Pearlman's *Infidelity* for $250,000 to Broadway—one of many major publishers that had initially rejected Pearlman's work of

168 · BEYOND FRUSTRATION

nonfiction. And it isn't just titles published by small houses that enjoy this satisfying fate. In many cases the same thing has happened to self-published books.

In the Tradition of Thoreau

A major trade publisher offered to buy Bill Branon's novel *Let Us Prey*, but only if he'd soften its tone. Instead, the retired Navy captain bought a handbook on self-publishing, shot a jacket picture in his garage, and spent $7,200 of his own money to print 5,000 copies of *Let Us Prey*. Branon then used his profits to keep going back to press. After 13,000 copies had been sold, HarperCollins bought the rights to Branon's self-published thriller for six figures.

With the help of sophisticated software, self-publishing has become a viable, attractive alternative for authors who can't tempt an established publisher or, like Bill Branon, would simply rather do it their way. A number of authors have turned down lucrative offers from publishers to successfully publish their own work (as Dickens did with *A Christmas Carol*). Stephen Wolfram spurned big publishers to self-publish his five-pound opus *A New Kind of Science*, which became an immediate bestseller. Dave Eggers (*A Heartbreaking Work of Staggering Genius*) self-published his novel *You Shall Know Our Velocity*, then sold it on his own Web site, bypassing even Amazon.

Self-publishing was once seen as a last resort by desperate writers. That was long ago. Thousands of books are now self-published every year, as many as 10 percent of all new titles. Modern technology makes it possible for self-publishers to produce attractive, professional-looking publications. (In time, "on-demand" presses will make it unnecessary for these authors to even clutter their attic, basement, or garage with unsold books.) As a result, there is now a flourishing subculture of self-published writers. They congregate at book fairs, street fairs, even county fairs, hawking their wares like summer squash and home-baked pies. I observe these author-merchants with mixed feelings. On the one hand, the quality of their literary product varies widely, as does the quality of their physical product. What they have in common is a determination to see their work in print and to put it in readers' hands. "There's information in here you'll find nowhere else," says the author of a book on Indian lore, tapping its cover like a preacher thumping his Bible. "Once you start reading my novel, you won't be able to put it down," a fiction writer assures a customer. That kind of zeal is hard not to admire. These authors could have said, as many do, "No one will publish me. I quit!" Or they could say, "To hell with them. If no one else will publish me, I'll publish myself!" And they do. And they take themselves and their work seriously enough to hawk it in the marketplace.

At the very least, publishing their own work gives authors sympathy for those they wish would do it for them (i.e., publishers). Even though I've never self-published, I did reprint a book of mine and found the process—from dealing with printers through marketing the book to schlepping heavy cartons to fulfilling orders and dunning deadbeats—most instructive. There are valuable lessons to be learned peddling one's own wares that way, not least being that you'd rather let someone else do it. The highlight, or lowlight, of my own experience was the 100-degree August day when a semi pulled up in front of my Ohio home. Its driver jumped down to the street, introduced himself, and said, "I've got a delivery for you."

"Of what?"

"Books."

"How many?"

"Sixteen hundred."

"Okay."

"Where's your forklift?"

"Forklift?"

"Yeah."

"What for?"

"To get these books off the truck."

"How are they packed?"

"Loose. On skids."

The upshot was that I had to round up some neighborhood kids and pay them to help me unload my books by hand and carry them—10 at a time—to my basement (where 1,000 or so are still stored).

This experience put me in the tradition of Henry David Thoreau. Thoreau said of the 706 copies of *A Week on the Concord and Merrimack Rivers* left over from a printing of 1,000 he'd paid for himself, "I now have a library of nearly nine hundred volumes, over seven hundred of which I wrote myself. They are something more successful than fame, as my back knows, which has borne them up two flights of stairs." Bringing out one's own work has a distinguished history. From *Leaves of Grass* to *The Christmas Box*, self-publishing has been a launching pad for countless successful books. After several publishers passed on Beatrix Potter's self-illustrated fable featuring a rabbit named Peter, she published the story herself. Once *The Tale of Peter Rabbit* was in print, a publisher who had previously turned her book down offered to reprint it if Potter would assume the financial risk. She did. *The Tale of Peter Rabbit* went on to become one of history's all-time bestselling books for children.

This is just one of many instances in which classic books began life as self-published ones. *Robert's Rules of Order* and *Bartlett's Familiar Quotations* were originally self-published, as was *Joy of Cooking*, when it was turned down by a number of publishers. After he spent a year in vain waiting for a response to his submission of *The Rubaiyat of Omar Khayyam*, Edward FitzGerald brought it out himself. Anaïs Nin not only self-published but self-*printed* her own early work until a rave review by Edmund Wilson caught the eye of major publishers. Even Proust had to pay to have his early work published, as did Virginia Woolf and Stephen Crane. When Crane could find no publisher for *Maggie: A Girl of the Streets*, he published it himself, under the pseudonym Johnson Smith. *Maggie* sold only 100 copies, and the poverty-stricken author was forced to use some unsold copies as fireplace fuel. Luckily, a prominent publisher happened on an unburned copy, contacted Crane, signed up *The Red Badge of Courage*, then reissued *Maggie* with great success.

One century later, a remarkable number of reviews have noted that the book being assessed was originally self-published. Hundreds of books that later appeared in publishers' catalogs were first brought out by their authors. Some, such as *Celestine Prophecy*, *The Christmas Box*, and *Mutant Message Down Under* were bought for eye-popping advances. Michael Hoeye's self-published *Time Stops for No Mouse* netted him a three-book contract with Penguin worth nearly $2 million. Any publisher's nightmare come true is having to pay a big advance for a self-published book it originally could have bought for a pittance, like the $4 million Simon & Schuster paid Richard Paul Evans for *The Christmas Box* and a follow-up. Ernest Callenbach's self-published novel *Ecotopia* was republished by Bantam—one of twenty publishers that originally turned it down. Other books that made their way from an author's garage to a publisher's warehouse include *Not a Day Goes By*, *The One Minute Manager*, *What Color Is Your*

Parachute?, *The Whole Earth Catalog*, *The Book of Questions*, *50 Simple Things You Can Do to Save the Earth*, *Leadership Secrets of Attila the Hun*, and *How to Avoid Probate*.

Then there are the novels of E. Lynn Harris. Harris had no more success than Stephen Crane did trying to get a publisher to accept the first one. Since the dozen editors who considered it seemed to think that fiction involving bisexual black men was double (if not triple) trouble, the thirty-nine-year-old computer salesman used what remained of his savings to print 5,000 copies of *Invisible Life*. He then loaded these books into his car and sold them at beauty salons and reading groups in the Atlanta area, as well as to small independent bookstores. Harris's novel stirred so much buzz around Atlanta that a Doubleday sales rep took note and brought the African-American novelist to the attention of an editor in the home office. At the same time, an agent to whom Harris had sent his self-published novel agreed to represent him. Seven novels later, Harris was a bestselling phenomenon with millions of books in print, all published by Doubleday.

For publishers, self-published books like Harris's have become market tests. Sales representatives from major houses troll bookstores looking for successful titles published by their own authors that their employers can reissue. Random House has given bonuses to reps who bring back promising self-published books. They consider them pretested. These books have already found an audience. By self-publishing them, their authors have demonstrated commitment. Since most live in the hinterlands, they reflect the tastes of the Great Out There. They don't just write *for* their audience; they *are* their audience. Buying books self-published by authors beyond the Hudson has become a way shrewd pub people at major trade houses compensate for their isolation. "If New York doesn't publish it, it doesn't mean it isn't good," said one Warner executive. "We're very bullish about self-publishing and small presses."

In some cases self-published books actually launch small presses. *When I Am an Old Woman I Shall Wear Purple* not only was self-published by Sandra Haldeman Martz in Watsonville, California, but became the basis for the Papier Mache Press, which Martz created to publish *Purple* and follow-up books. Like her, many a successful self-publisher has morphed into an actual publisher. The popular Zagat restaurant guides, for example, are still published by Tim and Nina Zagat because no trade publisher they solicited showed any interest in their project. Similarly, Vicki and Bruce Lansky founded Meadowbrook Press to publish Vicki's *Pre-Natal Cookbook*, then had a smash bestseller with its sequel, *Feed Me, I'm Yours!* The Lanskys' marriage did not survive, but the Meadowbrook Press did, and has become a well-regarded boutique publisher.

Self-publishing is not for the faint of heart. It requires a serious investment of money, time, energy, and ego. Most who engage in this activity don't even earn back their investment. But enough do to encourage the rest of us, and enough do well to fuel our dreams.

E-Publishing

Information technology is a Jekyll-Hyde presence in the lives of contemporary writers. Computers increase exponentially the volume of data besieging pub people. They contribute to the bottom-line emphasis of publishers, leaving no doubt how each book is "doing" commercially day-by-day, even hour-by-hour. Computers allow booksellers to determine in a keystroke how many *units* an author's last title sold, and order his next one accordingly. Many midlist authors who could have stayed afloat in a more vague commercial atmosphere can't survive this merciless record-keeping.

On the Jekyll side of the ledger, computers make writing itself infinitely easier and more malleable. They shorten the time it takes to produce a book (for better more than worse). They facilitate the submission process. E-mail, faxes, and Fed Ex make it easier for editors to consult writers about revisions, choice of title, jacket design, and whether to accept Oprah's invitation to appear on her show.

E-mail is the ideal communication medium for writers. Unlike talking on the phone, e-mail offers an opportunity to *edit*, to *revise*, and *polish* one's words before launching them into the judgmental world of dialogue. E-mail and the Internet also alleviate the loneliness of writing without the intrusiveness of a telephone's ring. Hardly a day goes by that I don't hear from a colleague, a reader, an editor, someone who wants to reprint something I've written, or buy one of my books, or wonders if Oscar Wilde actually said, "It is only the superficial who despise surfaces and appearances." (He didn't.)

Technology is the underlying reason that there has never been a better time to write and be read. It increases exponentially the tools writers have to reach readers. Reaching readers is all that really matters. How this happens is immaterial. The message is what counts, not the medium, and the future promises more media than ever for conveying one's message. We need to be thinking not just of how to get words onto paper but onto computer screens, Palm Pilots, Rocket Readers, CD-ROMs, MP3 files, and future forums that for now are just a fantasy of some kid tinkering in a garage.

Most writers dream of publishing an actual *book*, and should. This is our Mecca. But if we step back and think about it, isn't our more basic goal conveying our words, our thoughts, our inventions to the reading public? Books are one way to do this—a great way—but still only one. Somewhere between conventional books and those on-line are the version called *e-books*, ones downloaded from the Internet onto handheld readers. Even though e-books have not taken publishing by storm as many predicted they would, their sales have crept steadily upward. Along the way, writers and publishers have wasted inordinate amounts of time wondering if e-books will eventually replace printed books. Of course they won't. *Nothing* will replace printed books. They're irreplaceable, a marvelous vehicle for delivering text. Instead of asking whether printed books will disappear, we might better ask, "How will writing reach readers in the future?" Conventional books will certainly be one vehicle. E-books will be another. But their form will evolve into something quite different than books-on-a-screen.

Recall how automobiles evolved. Early versions looked like buckboard wagons with engines attached. It was decades before cars began to resemble a new mode of transportation altogether. Similarly, in its earliest incarnation, television was called "radio television." Early TV news broadcasters read copy before cameras, looking down at the paper in their hands, as if they were still in a radio studio. It took a couple of decades for television to become a medium all its own. The same thing will happen with e-books. Today they look like conventional books with a flicker. In time, just like cars and television, e-books will find their own form. Their length will vary more than conventional ones; they'll be shorter on average, with more graphics, more flexibility, more fluidity, and a wider range of prices. Short stories and novellas are better suited to the e-book format than novels. Articles and essays work better on their small screens than full-scale nonfiction books. E-books might be updated on a regular basis and perhaps incorporate reader feedback or author-reader dialogue. The possibilities are infinite and intriguing.

The Safety Net

The Internet could have been created with writers in mind. On its airwaves they chat with each other; access writer sites; do research; buy books (even obscure ones); check out publishers, agents, and the competition; set up Web sites; communicate with readers; publish their own writing; and sell the results. The Net has become a wide-open forum in which anyone can post work. For writers, it's a safety net where any project with even a few potential readers can be posted. The Internet is like one huge court of literary appeal for rejected, dejected writers. This is good news, very good. After all, getting published *per se* matters less than delivering one's words to readers. The Net provides yet another vehicle.

By making so many forums available for written words, perhaps the Net will reduce pressure to *publish* in conventional terms. At the same time, as with self-publishing, commercial publishers have begun to use on-line publication as an audition. Ever since M. J. Rose's novel *Lip Service* went from the Net onto Pocket Books's fiction list, any number of books have segued into hard copy after building an audience on-line.

Without the Internet, Zane, the bestselling author of erotic fiction for African-American women, might not have become a publishing phenomenon. Certainly that's her take. The author of *Addicted* and *The Heat Seekers* began writing stories with little thought of getting them published. Instead she just e-mailed them to friends. To Zane's surprise, not only her friends but friends of theirs began contacting the author, asking to see more. In response she posted new stories on her Web site, getting 8,000 hits in less than a month. This led Zane to create an e-mail newsletter that included still more stories. She then started selling her fiction in printed pages, culminating in a self-published novel. Major publishers caught wind of Zane's success and offered to reprint her novel, if she'd just make its sex a bit less explicit. Zane refused and kept selling her own work on-line, through street vendors, and, finally, in major bookstores. Her stellar sales record left publishers with no alternative. They hollered "Uncle!" and vied to republish Zane's work on her own terms. Pocket Books succeeded, and Zane has become a bestselling staple on its fiction list.

Far from threatening writers, information technology has opened up wondrous new ways for them to reach readers, publishers, and each other. At one time readers could only choose from a limited number of titles at small bookstores that were preselected by publishers. Now they have a far wider range of options: at big stores, on the Internet, from boutique publishers, self-publishers, and e-publishers. This strengthens writers. By making it possible to supplement or even bypass traditional publishing channels, information technology redresses somewhat the power imbalance between authors and publishers. Just as e-mail and the Internet eroded political tyrannies, they are putting more power in the hands of consumers, including readers, and those such as writers who would contact them directly.

In one visionary perspective, technology will eventually bridge the gap between writer and reader altogether. According to longtime editor Jason Epstein, it is only a matter of time before writer and reader dial direct. In *Book Business*, Epstein envisioned a digitized future where writers and readers no longer need publishers in the usual sense. Intermediaries between reader and writer will shrink, even vanish. Any writer who can post his or her work will have a shot in this marketplace. Publishing will then become a cottage industry, comprising loosely knit teams of editors, designers, publicists, and Web site managers.

In this brave new publishing world, print-on-demand (POD) will be more significant than e-books. Like vending machines brewing single cups of coffee, on-demand presses will produce books one at a time, whenever there's a customer ready to put a disk and a dollar in the slot. When enough machines that can print and bind single volumes are installed in Borders, Kinko's, Office Depot, Starbucks, perhaps even 7-Eleven, publishing will be transformed—to the benefit of writers. It is not inconceivable that POD machines will eventually become household items. Once this critical mass has been reached, it will become practical to ship books electronically rather than physically. That will drastically reduce, if not eliminate, the need for huge presses, warehouses, semis, forklifts, packing lists, invoices, and returns. This, in turn, will virtually eliminate the need to consider big upfront costs when determining whether to publish a book. Books with even modest readerships will become commercially viable. It will also mean that the shelf life of books will resemble that of Stonehenge monuments more than containers of Dannon yogurt. Books digitized for on-demand printing will never go out of print. Any book whose text has been uploaded will always be available for download. Once downloaded, it can be read on a monitor, printed out at home, or taken on a disk to one's friendly corner POD machine for an actual book to be produced.

Those invested in conventional ways of publishing won't embrace this change, of course. It will take time for everyone concerned—including writers and readers—to adjust. But the change is going to happen. And when it does, opportunities available to writers, and readers, will expand exponentially. Transformations in the publishing process will mean that any and all pieces of writing can be "published." This does not mean that all writing published this way will be read, of course. There are only so many readers and so many hours in the reading day. More published writing can't produce more readers with more time to read. What it will mean is that prescreening processes will be transformed. Now, this is largely done by agents, editors, and book reviewers, with help from reading group pickers. In the future, book buyers themselves will become the primary auditioning group. Preselection of book titles will be done by readers chatting on the Net and elsewhere more than by pub people. This shift will be comparable to the one in which candidates for high office were no longer chosen by politicians in smoke-filled rooms but by voters themselves during primary elections.

In the short run, readers will gravitate to what's actually readable. Over time, they'll discern what's genuinely valuable. "People have a profound instinct for quality," said Jason Epstein, "and yes they *can* tell good from bad." Once they have, they will want to discuss books they've judged to be good. Even those that don't benefit from loud drumbeats of publicity will enjoy free word of mouth on the Net and will be found easily by those Googling around looking for something good to read. Better Web sites will play the same role that better publishers do today: pre-assuring readers that worthwhile books can be found under their auspices. All of these factors constitute, in Epstein's understated conclusion, "grounds for optimism."

The Hopeful Writer

I am still encouraged to go on. I wouldn't know where
else to go.

E. B. White

Without my having soft-pedaled what you're up against, I
hope you realize by now how many tangible, realistic reasons
there are for writers to be hopeful. I have tried not to exaggerate
the prospects of publication. Mathematically speaking, those
odds aren't good. Only a minority of writers publish their work
in conventional media. But why assume at the outset that you
won't be one of them? Suppose John Grisham had assumed
that, or Terry McMillan, or J. K. Rowling?

Our sense of hope can't always be based on calculating
odds. It could hardly be otherwise in an activity that involves
trekking into the unknown. Writing seriously is more like
John Wesley Powell setting off down the Colorado without a
map than Jane Fonda as Lillian Hellman in the movie *Julia*,
banging typewriter keys furiously with Dashiell Hammett at
her side, cheering her on.

Harrowing as it can be, writing is also one of the most
gratifying activities one can undertake—in part because it is so
harrowing. Even the knowledge that writers must buck stiff
odds is not without its appeal. People sometimes ask me if I
gamble. I do, I respond. I write.

Divers

At the age of thirty-five, a friend of mine named Jeff left his job as a microbiologist to become a freelance writer. Within months he'd sold articles to several publications, including two of national prominence. Jeff seemed to be on his way. He was enjoying more success than I had at that stage of my career. The next thing I knew, Jeff had returned to his old job. What happened to his writing dream? Jeff told me he hadn't met his projections. He'd plotted a curve in advance that charted the progress he hoped to make. Not having risen far enough fast enough on this curve, Jeff threw in his hand and went back to microbiology.

That's the approach of a scientist, not a writer. Writers don't plot career paths. They set out for the territories with a Snickers bar in their fanny pack and a half-filled canteen of water. Jeff couldn't do that. It wasn't lack of ability or skill that drove him from the ranks of writers; it was lack of daring and will.

It's hard to be a writer without recklessness and resolve. Authors sometimes compare themselves to explorers like Lewis and Clark. Certainly, they have more in common with that group than, say, literature professors. They need no more risk in their life than putting words on paper. The siren call of adventure is part of what lures writers. Except their brand of adventure can be more hazardous than the kind that usually goes by this name. "Writing a first-rate book is no easier than climbing Mount Everest," said editor-author William Targ. "I think Everest is easier."

Writers choose the most dangerous path of all: the one that leads inward, into the unmapped caverns of their secret selves. How daring can you get? "I love all men who *dive!*" said Melville, referring to the inner expedition every writer must undertake. Deep satisfaction comes from doing something this bold, with an outcome so uncertain. Anxiety goes with this territory. Anxious writers who write anyway feel more pride than shame, and should. One thing that makes writing rewarding is the very fact that it *is* so scary. If this weren't an anxious business, where would the satisfaction be? The challenge? The excitement? Even writers who don't publish, or who do publish but are not as successful as they'd wish, have engaged in one of the most daring and rewarding acts available to man- and womankind.

The Common Thread

A retired college professor who lives in my town began calling me a few years ago to discuss her memoir-in-progress. I always knew it was Mathilde on the phone because of the muted, if-you're-too-busy-this-can-wait tone of her voice. If ever an aspiring writer sounded likely to toss in the towel, it was Mathilde. Ordinarily, I do everything I can to get such callers off the line and imply politely that they shouldn't call back. But beneath all the excuses and apologies I sensed something else. Sure enough, no matter how hard I tried to discourage her, Mathilde kept calling, kept asking me questions, kept soliciting and taking my advice about submitting her memoir to agents and publishers. In time—years, actually—it was published by a university press.

If any thread connects the many authors I've discussed in this book, it is this: *They don't give up easily.* The determination of your average working writer would impress Sir Edmund Hillary. It's the secret of their success. That and an ability to take a punch. "The true novelist must be at once driven and indifferent," wrote John Gardner. By this he meant driven to produce works of art, while remaining philosophical about their fate. "Van Gogh never sold a painting in his life," Gardner pointed out. "Poe came close with poetry and fiction, selling very little. Drivenness only helps if it forces the writer not to suicide but to the making of splendid works of art, allowing him indifference to whether or not the novel sells, whether or not it's appreciated."

Even those who complete a manuscript that doesn't get published—even one that doesn't *deserve* to get published—have pulled off an awesome feat. That is why I've made so little attempt in this book to assess the product of writing, as opposed to the process. This is for a reason. It's not that I consider *Moby Dick* and *Mutant Message Down Under* to be equivalent. Rather, it's that I do consider the act of writing, coping with frustration, dealing with editors, and confronting despair to be comparable among writers of all kinds.

Authors realize this. Like athletes on opposing teams, they can be remarkably sympathetic to those running the same race, regardless of how clumsy their gait. Any number of writers have made this point, often quoting Aldous Huxley's observation in his novel *Point Counter Point* that "a bad book is as much of a labour to write as a good one; it comes as sincerely from the author's soul."

While completing *Madame Bovary*, Flaubert grew intrigued with the story of a man he knew who was now confined to an insane asylum, raving, screaming, and being plunged into cold baths to try to stop him from screaming and raving. A year earlier Flaubert had read a book of poetry written by this man. Even though the poems themselves weren't very good, Flaubert was moved by the "sincerity, enthusiasm, and faith" displayed by their author. "It is a delicious thing to write," he observed, "whether well or badly."

No Ex-writers

Writing has rewards all its own. Perhaps that is why, as someone once observed, you so seldom meet an ex-writer. Sure, we would all like to have our work published (most of us, anyway), published well, and have our work recognized. Few of us would object if our writing earned money, even lots of money. But that's not why an actual writer writes. An actual writer writes because he or she doesn't have much choice. Authors repeatedly say that if they felt they could choose, they might choose to do something else. Yet some of these very same writers will also say that no other activity gives them the same sense of satisfaction. Even though she found writing "frightfully hard work," Katherine Anne Porter said that while doing it she experienced "a joy as nearly pure as I expect to have on this earth." In her memoir, *Landscapes of the Heart*, novelist Elizabeth Spencer wrote of "magical days" when her writing seemed to flow, when she never wanted to stop, when she would pause to glance at the clock and realize it said three o'clock and she was hungry, but even more than hungry she was *happy*.

Like athletes, mystics, chess players, rock climbers, dancers, and painters, writers routinely enter a trancelike state. That state has something in common with erotic ecstasy. More than one author has compared the complete absorption of writing to that of making love, and the sense of contentment they experience afterward as a form of afterglow. Novelist Lee Smith said that when her writing goes well, "my every sense is keen and quivering." The excitement this produces is physical, said Smith, "almost sexual."

Lee Smith also compared the exhilaration of writing to the sense of edgy holiness that a religious snake handler once described to her. Authors commonly portray the act of writing in quasi-religious terms. Kafka and others considered writing a form of worship. To them, it was a calling. John Gardner called his chosen vocation a "way," one whose profits were primarily spiritual. "For those who are authentically called to the profession," said Gardner, "spiritual profits are enough."

The Joy of Writing

After I spoke at a writing conference in Columbus, Ohio, a schoolteacher named Tom approached me to discuss a book of mine that he had read. What kind of writing do you do? I asked him.

"Short stories," Tom replied.

"Are you trying to get them published?"

"Not really," he said.

"Why not?"

"Why should I?" Tom asked. "The only two reasons I can think of to publish are money and fame. I already make a decent salary, and just about everyone in the town where I live knows who I am. That's fame enough for me. So I just write for my own enjoyment." I thought Tom's priorities were in remarkably good order.

Some write for their own eyes only, or perhaps those of a few confidants. This could be the purest form of writing: at their own behest, for their own satisfaction, without regard for publishers they fear and readers they don't know. They may have decided that the grail of publishing is not worth the freezing mountains and suffocating deserts they must cross to get there. This conclusion could free them to do some very good writing.

Publishing one's work is only one measure of success. There are many others, gratifications for writing that some consider beyond mere publication. That was how Emily Dickinson regarded the act of writing poetry. Even though there was little doubt that her verse was publishable, Dickinson thought that seeing her work or her name in print had nothing to do with the act of composition. After publishing one poem anonymously in an Amherst literary magazine, she stopped submitting her verse and declined friends' offers to do so for her. Why? Dickinson's biographers have puzzled over this question since her death in 1886, at the age of fifty-six. "They'd advertise," she fretted in one poem. In another Dickinson contended that "Publication—is the Auction / Of the Mind of Man." Emily Dickinson was content to sew her poems into one-of-a-kind chapbooks and share them with friends. Her biographer, Alfred Habegger, concluded that she simply didn't want to accept the consequences of becoming a public person. Only after her work appeared in print posthumously did the recluse become a celebrity. "We may suspect," wrote Habegger, "the poet would have seen her lasting fame as a contemptible substitute for the limitlessness and perfection she had spent her life thinking about."

Although Dickinson may have been the most committed of nonpublishing writers, many of her colleagues—even published ones—shared the poet's disdain for publication. Noted writers of all kinds consider seeing their words in print a mere by-product of the inherent rewards for recording them. Even though he began writing at eleven, Flaubert resisted the urge to publish until he was thirty-five. Flaubert characterized publication of one's writing as "the height of prostitution, and the vilest kind." The author of *Madame Bovary* was not consistent on this point, of course. Recall his advice about courting editors. After resolving to publish, he worked diligently to get his own novels in print. At the same time, Flaubert retained his conviction that writing was best done for its own sake. He considered books to be an organic part of their creators, something that could be made public only by tearing "a length of gut from our bellies and serv[ing] it up to the bourgeois. Drops of our hearts' blood are visible in every letter we trace. But once our work is printed—farewell! It belongs to everyone. The crowd tramples on us."

Spit in the Face of Despair

Let's say you pursue every alternative for conventional publication we've explored in this book, to no avail, and prefer not to self-publish or e-publish your work. Is that it for you as a writer? Hardly. In the tradition of Emily Dickinson, you may find that some of your most satisfying work is writing you don't intend to make public. Words written for their own sake have a unique appeal. Some of my own favorite writing may be unpublishable. In particular the family memoir I spent the better part of a year researching and writing will probably never appear in print. So be it. I wrote that memoir exactly the way I wanted, with no thought of the marketplace. In it I discussed freely the uncle who committed suicide rather than come out of the closet; my Tanta Karolina, who was said to have run a brothel in Saigon before becoming a fortune-teller in Bucharest; and a cousin in Philadelphia who died at twenty-two of a botched abortion, even though seeing this in print would have devastated her only living sibling, a brother who has since passed on. Researching this family history taught me a lot about my relatives that I could have learned no other way. Writing about them gave structure, focus, and depth to my family's saga. And—because I didn't approach it with publishing in mind—I was free to write as honestly as I could, without publisher-courting strategies that might distort the truth as I saw it. Even though it's unlikely that the results will ever earn an ISBN number, I'm glad I wrote that memoir.

So why did I write it? And why do so many writers keep

tapping their keyboards or scribbling on legal pads with so little prospect of publication? The desire to be read is a good reason for writing, but only one. There are many others. Kingsley Amis said he wrote primarily to entertain himself. That's why Margaret Mitchell said she wrote *Gone with the Wind*. Pat Conroy's stated goal is to explain his own life to himself. Many of his colleagues have made similar observations. "In a very real sense," said Alfred Kazin, "the writer writes in order to teach himself, to understand himself, to satisfy himself; the publishing of his ideas, though it brings gratification, is a curious anticlimax."

Authors routinely say they write to explore their inner world. This prospect is precisely what scares off many a would-be writer. According to John Cheever's son Ben, his father used to say disdainfully that some people were afraid to write a business letter for fear of encountering themselves. That wasn't John Cheever's problem. "He couldn't write a postcard without encountering himself," his son observed. "But he'd write the postcard anyway. He'd encounter himself, transform himself, and you'd have a hell of a postcard."

In the process of discovering things about themselves, writers jettison ones that are weighing them down. Nobel Prize winner Kenzaburo Oe described writing his novels as "a way of exorcising demons." D. H. Lawrence talked of "shedding one's sicknesses in books." Writing, concluded Terry McMillan, "forces me to face and understand my flaws and weaknesses and strength. . . . It has become my way of responding to and dealing with things I find too disturbing or distressing or painful to handle in any other way."

The writing process hasn't been subjected to much research, which is probably just as well. In a rare exception, however, a group of patients who suffered from serious asthma or arthritis were given an opportunity to write about traumatic experiences:

an auto accident, say, the death of a loved one, or getting fired from a job. Four months later, those who spent a single hour doing this type of writing had improved both emotionally and physically significantly more than another group of patients who had been told simply to write about their plans for the day. Similar studies have had comparable results. Apparently, the act of writing about matters of personal significance has health-giving properties.

That's certainly been my experience. Do I wish I'd been more popular in high school? Write a book about it. Would I like to be taller? Excellent fodder for another book. So was my curiosity about who took risks and why, and why I didn't take more risks myself. In the process of exploring such topics on paper, I lightened their load in my psyche.

"Writing is a form of therapy," said Graham Greene. "Sometimes I wonder how all those who do not write, compose or paint can manage to escape the madness, the melancholia, the panic fear which is inherent in the human condition." When they talk of writing as therapy—and many do—writers don't use that term in a vague or allegorical way. Writing escorts them inside their head so they can root around in the mess. This process is rather like shining a flashlight in a cluttered, dark, somewhat ominous old closet to see what's there, then straightening things up and hauling what's trash to the landfill. Stephen King has repeatedly said that's how writing has kept him sane. King, an unusually phobic person with obsessive-compulsive tendencies, said his chosen profession allows him to throw out his psychological garbage. "As a writer," he explained, "I can externalize my fears and insecurities and night terrors on paper, which is what people pay shrinks a small fortune to do. In my case, they pay me for psychoanalyzing myself in print."

King gave another, related reason for his chosen vocation.

He thought writing was an amulet, a way to "spit in the face of the despair." In other words, one reason we write is *because* we're desperate. The act of writing helps us confront our sense of desperation, understand it, lighten its load, and muddle through.

This brings us full circle. We began by considering the anxiety, frustration, and despair that is an inherent part of the writing process. We've examined a wide range of ways to deal with this syndrome. The best way of all can be found in writing itself. Writing is both a cause of despair and an antidote to despair. Put another way, on days when we're feeling hopeless, the best way to revive our sense of hope is to keep on writing.

Notes

Uncited comments and anecdotes come from off-the-record interviews, personal conversations, or speeches attended by the author.

1. The Essential Ingredient

3   Grisham: *People*, March 16, 1992; *Publishers Weekly*, February 22, 1993, and January 19, 1998; *Atlanta Constitution*, March 7, 1993; *Current Biography Yearbook*, 1993; *Entertainment Weekly*, April 1, 1994; *USA Today*, June 2, 1994; Mary Beth Pringle, *John Grisham: A Critical Companion* (Westport, Conn.: Greenwood Press, 1997); Robyn M. Weaver, *John Grisham* (San Diego: Lucent Books, 1999); *Newsweek*, February 15, 1999; *New York Times*, February 4, 2002; *Fresh Air* (National Public Radio), February 8, 2002.

4–5   Lamott: Anne Lamott, *Bird by Bird: Some Instructions on Writing and Life* (New York: Pantheon, 1994), 19; "How to Be a Writer," Salon.com, 1999.

5   King: Stephen King, *On Writing: A Memoir of the Craft* (New York: Scribner, 2000), 248.

5–6   Bellow-Wasserman: Harriet Wasserman, *Handsome Is: Adventures with Saul Bellow* (New York: Fromm International, 1997), 66.

6   Busch: Frederick Busch, *A Dangerous Profession: A Book about the Writing Life* (New York: St. Martin's, 1998; Broadway, 1999), 73.

7–8   Barrett-Prashker-Van Wormer: John F. Baker, *Literary Agents: A Writer's Introduction* (New York: Macmillan, 1999), 16.

8   . Lerner: Betsy Lerner, *The Forest for the Trees: An Editor's Advice to Writers* (New York: Riverhead, 2000), 34, 32.

8   Garrett: *Inside UVA Online*, December 10, 1999–January 13, 2000.

9   Jonellen Heckler's novels are: *Safekeeping* (New York: Putnam's, 1983; Fawcett, 1984); *A Fragile Peace* (New York: Putnam's, 1986; Pocket, 1987); *White Lies* (New York: Putnam's, 1989); *Circumstances Unknown* (New York: Pocket, 1994); *Final Tour* (New York: Pocket, 1996).

9   Gardner: John Gardner, *On Becoming a Novelist* (New York: Norton, 1983; reprint, 1999), xxiv.

12–13 Godwin: National Book Award authors, *The Writing Life: A Collection of Essays and Interviews* (New York: Random House, 1995), 10.

13   Grisham: See previous citations for Grisham, p. 191.

2. AFD Syndrome

14   Conrad: Donald M. Murray, *Shoptalk: Learning to Write with Writers* (Portsmouth, N.H.: Boynton/Cook, 1990), 49–50.

14   Percy: Ibid., 28.

15   Grafton: presentation to the Antioch Writers' Workshop, July 11, 1990.

16   Canin: *New York Times*, November 10, 1998.

16   Godwin: National Book Award Authors, *The Writing Life*, 5, 8.

16   Didion: *New York Times Book Review*, April 3, 1977.

16   Cheever: John Cheever, *The Journals of John Cheever* (New York: Knopf, 1991), 13, 22, 29.

16   Baxter: Frederick Busch, ed., *Letters to a Fiction Writer* (New York: Norton, 1999), 47, 49.

16   Steel: *New York Times Book Review*, March 8, 1987.

16–17 Fitzgerald to Perkins: Matthew J. Bruccoli and Judith S. Baughman, ed., *F. Scott Fitzgerald on Authorship* (Columbia, S.C.: University of South Carolina Press, 1996), 93, 97.

17   Amis: *Publishers Weekly*, February 8, 1985.

19   Mailer: *Charlie Rose* (Public Broadcasting System), September 10, 1995.

19   King: King, *On Writing*, 209.

19   Munro: *New York Times*, November 30, 1998; "A Conversation with Alice Munro," undated, Reading Group Center (The Reading Group Source, Vintage Books, Anchor Books), on-line; Thomas E. Tausky, "Alice Munro: Biocritical Essay," Canadian

Literary Archives, University of Calgary Library, 1986; Alice Munro, "Cortes Island," in *The Love of a Good Woman* (New York: Knopf, 1998), 124. See also: *Publishers Weekly*, August 22, 1986; *Current Biography Yearbook*, 1990; Catherine Sheldrick Ross, *Alice Munro: A Double Life* (Toronto: ECW Press, 1992); "Alice Munro: The Art of Fiction," *Paris Review*, vol. 36, no. 131 (1994); *Newsweek*, October 21, 1996; *Atlantic Monthly*, December 2001; Atlantic Unbound, *Atlantic Online*, December 14, 2001; *New Republic*, February 23, 2002.

21 Singer: *New York Times*, January 22, 1986.

21 Roth: George Plimpton, ed., *Writers at Work*, 7th ser. (New York: Viking, 1986), 271.

21 Mann: Murray in Murray, *Shoptalk*, 194; *Washington Independent Writers Newsletter*, May 1978; Baxter in Busch, *Letters to a Fiction Writer*, 50; George Plimpton, ed., *The Writer's Chapbook: A Compendium of Fact, Opinion, Wit, and Advice from the 20th Century's Preeminent Writers* (New York: Viking, 1989), iv.

21 One author: Bob Olmstead to Lee Abbott in Busch, *Letters to a Fiction Writer*, 17.

22 Perkins to Hale: John Hall Wheelock, ed., *Editor to Author: The Letters of Maxwell E. Perkins* (New York: Universal Library, 1950), 127, 191; A. Scott Berg, *Max Perkins: Editor of Genius* (New York: Dutton, 1978; Pocket, 1979), 260.

22–23 Roethke: Carol Edgarian and Tom Jenks, *The Writer's Life: Intimate Thoughts on Work, Love, Inspiration, and Fame from the Diaries of the World's Great Writers* (New York: Vintage, 1997), 20.

23 Toole-Percy: introduction to John Toole, *A Confederacy of Dunces* (Baton Rouge: Louisiana State University Press, 1980; Black Cat, 1981), 11–13; *People*, August 22, 1980; *Publishers Weekly*, March 20, 2000.

24 Manchester: essay by William Manchester in John Dorsey, *On Mencken* (New York: Knopf, 1980), 5.

24 Flaubert: Francis Steegmuller, ed., *The Selected Letters of Gustave Flaubert* (New York: Farrar Straus & Giroux, 1953; reprinted by Books for Libraries Press, 1971), 128, 131, 174.

24 Mencken: H. L. Mencken, *Minority Report: H. L. Mencken's Notebooks* (New York: Knopf, 1956), 19.

25–26 Woolf: Leonard Woolf, ed., *A Writer's Diary* (New York: Harcourt Brace Jovanovich, 1953), 25.

26 Ozick: *New York Times Magazine*, April 10, 1983; *Current Biography Yearbook*, 1983; *New York Times Book Review*, July 21, 1985;

Publishers Weekly, March 27, 1987; George Plimpton, ed., *Writers at Work*, 8th ser. (New York: Viking, 1988), 195–223.

27   Flaubert to Colet: *The Selected Letters of Gustave Flaubert*, 148.

27   Gass: George Plimpton, ed., *Writers at Work*, 5th ser. (New York: Viking, 1981), 273.

27   Davies: Susan Shaughnessy, *Walking on Alligators: A Book of Meditations for Writers* (San Francisco: HarperSanFrancisco, 1993), 8.

3. Dealing with Discouragers

29   Jance: J. A. Jance, *Devil's Claw* (New York: Morrow, 2000), 241–42.

29   Bagehot: Walter Bagehot, *Literary Studies*, vol. 1 (1879; reprint, New York: Dutton, 1951), 152.

30   MacLachlan: *Dayton Daily News*, December 2, 1994.

30   Bombeck: Ibid., April 23, 1996.

30   Ellison: George Beahm, *The Stephen King Companion* (Kansas City, Mo.: Andrews and McMeel, 1983), 146.

30   Gallant: Mavis Gallant, *The Selected Short Stories of Mavis Gallant* (Toronto: McClelland & Stewart, 1996), x.

30   Fitzgerald: Bruccoli and Baughman, *F. Scott Fitzgerald on Authorship*, 39.

30   Atwood: Margaret Atwood, *Negotiating with the Dead: A Writer on Writing* (Cambridge, Eng.: Cambridge University Press, 2002), 108.

31   Atwood's brother: Ibid., 16.

31   Atwood: Ibid., 26.

31   Hoagland's parents: *Publishers Weekly*, March 19, 2001.

32   Wharton's parents: *New York Times Magazine*, April 10, 1983.

32   Turow's mother: *Time*, June 11, 1990; Kay Bonetti, Greg Michalson, Speer Morgan, Jo Sapp, and Sam Stowers, eds., *Conversations with American Novelists: The Best Interviews from The Missouri Review and the American Audio Prose Library* (Columbia, Mo.: University of Missouri Press, 1997), 154.

32   Martin's father: *New Yorker*, June 17–24, 2002.

32   poll: Jenkins Group, Inc., press release, PRNewswire, September 23, 2002; *New York Times*, September 28, 2002; *Dayton Daily News*, October 6, 2002.

32–33   Beattie: Busch, *Letters to a Fiction Writer*, 55.

33   Chekhov: *Authors Guild Bulletin*, Fall 2000.

35 Patchett: Will Blythe, *Why I Write: Thoughts on the Craft of Fiction* (Boston: Little, Brown, 1998), 62.

35 Ozick: *Current Biography Yearbook*, 1983, 280; Plimpton, *Writers at Work*, 8th ser., 217–18.

35 Willamson: *Newsweek*, August 23, 1999.

36 Grafton: *Modern Maturity*, July–August 1995.

36 Baxter: Busch, *Letters to a Fiction Writer*, 46.

37 King: Larry L. King, *None But a Blockhead: On Being a Writer* (New York: Viking, 1986), 18–19, 252–53.

37 Alther: *New York Times*, January 16, 1981.

38 Steinbeck: James Atlas, *Bellow: A Biography* (New York: Random House, 2000), 463.

38 Wolfe: Berg, *Max Perkins: Editor of Genius*, 336.

38 Solotaroff: Theodore Solotaroff, *A Few Good Voices in My Head: Occasional Pieces on Writing, Editing, and Reading My Contemporaries* (New York: Harper & Row, 1987), 67.

4. Exorcising Excuses

40 Shields: Carol Shields, *Unless* (New York: HarperCollins, 2002), 42.

40 cartoon: *New Yorker*, November 26, 2001.

40–41 Clark: Mary Higgins Clark, *Kitchen Privileges: A Memoir* (New York: Simon & Schuster, 2002); *McCall's*, November 1977; *People*, March 6, 1978; *New York Times Book Review*, May 14, 1978; *Philadelphia Inquirer*, July 18, 1980, August 7, 1988; *Current Biography Yearbook*, 1994; *Dayton Daily News*, May 23, 1995, April 5, 1996.

41 Patchett: *Publishers Weekly*, October 13, 1997.

42 LeGuin: *Writer's Digest*, May 2001.

42 King: Beahm, *The Stephen King Companion*, 25; Stephen King, *Secret Windows: Essays and Fiction on the Craft of Writing* (New York: Book-of-the-Month Club, 2000), 43.

42 Baldwin: Plimpton, *The Writer's Chapbook*, 49.

42 Shields: *Publishers Weekly*, February 28, 1994; *People*, June 26, 1995; *New York Times*, April 14, 2002; *Fresh Air* (National Public Radio), May 1, 2002; *Time*, May 27, 2002.

43 Trollope: Anthony Trollope, *Autobiography of Anthony Trollope* (New York: Dodd, Mead, 1905), 103–5.

43 Grafton: presentation to the Antioch Writers' Workshop, July 11, 1990.

43 Grisham: See previous citations for Grisham, p. 191.

43   Yerby: *New York Times Book Review*, June 13, 1982.

43   Christie: Agatha Christie, *Agatha Christie: An Autobiography* (New York: Dodd, Mead, 1977; Ballantine, 1978), 590–91, 617; Sophy Burnham, *For Writers Only* (New York: Ballantine, 1996), 113, 115.

43   Edson: *Time*, April 26, 1999.

43   Curtis: Ibid., January 31, 2000.

43   Turow: Ibid., June 11, 1990; Bonetti et al., *Conversations with American Novelists*, 154.

43–44   hooks: bell hooks, *remembered rapture: the writer at work* (New York: Henry Holt, 1999), 170, 172.

44   Grisham: *Publishers Weekly*, February 22, 1993.

44   Williams: Hilma Wolitzer in Busch, *Letters to a Fiction Writer*, 259.

44   Chekhov: *New York Times*, August 22, 2000.

44–45   Larkin: Andrew Motion, *Philip Larkin: A Writer's Life* (New York: Farrar Straus & Giroux, 1993), 490; Plimpton, *Writers at Work*, 7th ser., 158.

45   Rienstra: *Publishers Weekly*, February 25, 2002.

45   Tolstoy: Edgarian and Jenks, *The Writer's Life*, 181.

45   Flaubert: *The Selected Letters of Gustave Flaubert*, 85.

46   Greene: Murray, *Shoptalk*, 54.

46   Brown: Bonetti et al., *Conversations with American Novelists*, 250.

46   Heller: George Plimpton, ed., *Writers at Work*, 5th ser., 240.

46   Garrett: Busch, *Letters to a Fiction Writer*, 168.

47   Friedman: Bonnie Friedman, *Writing Past Dark: Envy, Fear, Distraction, and Other Dilemmas in the Writer's Life* (New York: HarperCollins, 1993), xiii.

47   A manager of musicians: *New York Times*, February 19, 1984.

47   Berryman: Plimpton, *Writers at Work*, 4th ser. (New York: Viking, 1976), 322.

47   Research on music students: *New Yorker*, December 17, 2001.

47   willingness to practice: Ibid., January 28, 2002.

47   Lerner: Lerner, *The Forest for the Trees*, 33.

48   Grimes: *Washington Post*, November 30, 1999.

48   Gardner: Gardner, *On Becoming a Novelist*, 70.

48   Solotaroff: Solotaroff, *A Few Good Voices in My Head*, 54.

48–49   Chase: *New York Times*, January 10, 1987.

49   Baxter: Busch, *Letters to a Fiction Writer*, 40.

49   Maugham: *Authors Guild Bulletin*, March–May 1977.

50   Faulkner: George Plimpton, ed., *Writers at Work*, 1st ser. (New York: Viking, 1958), 134.

50   Kennedy: Plimpton, *The Writer's Chapbook*, 38.

50   Yerby: *New York Times Book Review*, June 13, 1982.
50   France: Kenneth Atchity, *A Writer's Time: A Guide to the Creative Process, from Vision through Revision* (New York: Norton, 1986), 181.
50   Brown: Bonetti et al., *Conversations with American Novelists*, 249, 253.
50   Lessing: Jon Winokur, ed., *Writers on Writing* (Philadelphia: Running Press, 1987), 89.
51   Fowles: Murray, *Shoptalk*, 183.
51   O'Connor: *Newsweek*, September 7, 1981.
51   Hemingway: George Plimpton, ed., *Writers at Work*, 2nd ser. (New York: Viking, 1963), 224.
51–52 Perelman: Ibid., 248.
52   Hall: *People*, October 18, 1993.
52   Vidal: *Writer*, October 1976.
52   Brown: Busch, *Letters to a Fiction Writer*, 93.
52–53 Prowell: Amazon Books interview with Sandra West Prowell, amazon.com; *Publishers Weekly*, July 11, 1994.
53   Flagg: Ibid., September 21, 1998.
53   Columbia study: Paul William Kingston and Jonathan R. Cole, *Wages of Writing* (New York: Columbia University Press, 1986), 72–73.
54–55 Turow: *New York Times Magazine*, June 7, 1987; *Barrister*, Summer 1988; *Philadelphia Inquirer*, July 30, 1987; *Time*, June 11, 1990; *Current Biography Yearbook*, 1991; Sybil Steinberg, ed., *Writing for Your Life* (Wainscott, N.Y.: Pushcart Press, 1992), 507–11; Bonetti et al., *Conversations with American Novelists*, 156, 162; *Authors Guild Bulletin*, Spring 2000.
55   Lodge: David Lodge, *The Practice of Writing* (London: Allen Lane / Penguin, 1997), 176.
55   Vidal: Jay Parini, *Some Necessary Angels: Essays on Writing and Politics* (New York: Columbia University Press, 1997), 234.
56   Ludlum reviewer: *Newsweek*, March 26, 2001.
56   Prose: *Fresh Air* (National Public Radio), May 1, 2000.
59   Kempthorne-Foveaux: *Iowa Alumni Quarterly*, Autumn 1997; *LifeStory Magazine*, undated, issues #47, 55; *Time*, November 8, 1999.
59   Barron: *Psychology Today*, July 1972; *Human Behavior*, January 1979.
59–60 A sociologist: *Gerontologist*, Winter 1972.
60   Kempthorne: *Iowa Alumni Quarterly*, Autumn 1997.

60   Drucker: *New York Times Book Review*, May 23, 1982.

60   McCourt: *USA Today*, March 18, 1997.

60–61   Shields: *People*, June 26, 1995.

61   Godwin: "A Writing Woman," *Atlantic Monthly*, October 1979, reprinted as "Becoming a Writer," in Janet Sternburg, ed., *The Writer on Her Work* (New York: Norton, 1980), 253.

61   Welty: Michael Kreyling, *Author and Agent: Eudora Welty and Diarmuid Russell* (New York: Farrar Straus & Giroux, 1991), 73.

61   Murdoch novel: Iris Murdoch, *The Black Prince* (New York: Viking, 1973), 141.

61   Burgess: *New York Times*, April 12, 1981.

62   Didion: Plimpton, *Writers at Work*, 5th ser., 344.

62   Massello: Robert Massello, *Writer Tells All: Insider Secrets to Getting Your Book Published* (New York: Holt/Owl, 2001), 116.

62–63   Marcos: *New York Times*, August 5, 1983.

63   Ladd: *National Enquirer*, December 13, 1977.

63   Melville: *Dayton Daily News*, April 26, 1996.

64   Faulkner: *New York Times*, December 17, 1950.

5. Rites of Rejection

67   Gardner: Gardner, *On Becoming a Novelist*, 104.

67   Herman: Jeff Herman, *Writer's Guide to Book Editors, Publishers, and Literary Agents 2001–2002* (Roseville, Calif.: Prima Publishing, 2000), 737.

68   LeGuin: *Writer's Digest*, May 2001.

68   Burke: Baker, *Literary Agents*, 217.

68   Donleavy: James Charlton and Lisbeth Mark, *The Writer's Home Companion: Anecdotes, Comforts, Recollections and Other Amusements for Every Writer, Editor and Reader* (New York: Franklin Watts, 1987), 26; Massello, *Writer Tells All*, 106.

68   Knowles: George Plimpton, *Truman Capote* (New York: Doubleday, 1997), 237.

68–69   Salinger: *New Yorker*, October 1, 2001; Ben Yagoda, *About Town: The New Yorker and the World It Made* (New York: Scribner, 2000), 236.

69   Ozick: Ibid., 18–19.

69   Munro: *New York Times*, November 30, 1998.

69   Thurber-Mosher: James Thurber, *The Years with Ross* (Boston: Atlantic Monthly Press, 1959), 33.

69   Yagoda: Yagoda, *About Town*, 18.

69   Beattie: Ibid., 22–23, 384–88; Ben Yagoda on *Booknook*, WYSO-FM (Yellow Springs, Ohio), March 7, 2000.

69   Carver: Yagoda, *About Town*, 390.

70   Salinger: Yagoda, *About Town*, 233–36; J. D. Salinger, *Nine Stories* (Boston: Little, Brown, 1953; New American Library, 1954).

70–71   *Chicken Soup*: Herman, *Writer's Guide to Book Editors, Publishers, and Literary Agents 2001–2002*, 738–39.

71   Toole: *New York Times*, August 22, 2000; *Fresh Air* (National Public Radio), September 12, 2002.

72   Solotaroff: Solotaroff, *A Few Good Voices in My Head*, 62.

72   Dubus: Busch, *Letters to a Fiction Writer*, 139.

72   Fitzgerald: Bruccoli and Baughman, *F. Scott Fitzgerald on Authorship*, 39.

72   Rukeyser: Andre Bernard, ed., *Rotten Rejections: A Literary Companion* (Wainscott, N.Y.: Pushcart Press, 1990), 45.

73   King: Tim Underwood and Chuck Miller, eds., *Bare Bones: Conversations on Terror with Stephen King* (New York: McGraw-Hill, 1988), 73.

73   cummings: e.e. cummings, *No Thanks* (1935; reprint, New York: Liveright, 1978).

73   Kertesz: BBC News, October 10, 2002; *New York Times*, October 11, 2002.

74   Irving: Christopher Cerf and Victory Navasky, *The Experts Speak: The Definitive Compendium of Authoritative Misinformation* (New York: Villard, 1998), 180–81; *New York Times Book Review*, July 21, 1985.

74   Some Web sites: *New York Times*, January 11, 2001.

74   Gutman: Ibid.

74   Singer: *New York Times Book Review*, July 21, 1985.

74–75   Bellow: Ibid.; Atlas, *Bellow*, 231; Wasserman, *Handsome Is*, 164–65.

75   King: Underwood and Miller, *Bare Bones*, 72–73; *New York Times Book Review*, July 21, 1985.

75   Belloc: Clifton Fadiman, ed., *The Little, Brown Book of Anecdotes* (Boston: Little, Brown, 1985), 51.

76   Graves: Plimpton, *Writers at Work*, 4th ser., 65.

76   Moore: Donald Hall, ed., *The Oxford Book of American Literary Anecdotes* (New York: Oxford University Press, 1981), 218.

76   Wolitzer: Busch, *Letters to a Fiction Writer*, 255.

76–77   Cunningham: *Publishers Weekly*, November 2, 1998.

77–78   Cannell: *People*, June 5, 1995; *Dayton Daily News*, September 12, 1999; *Newsweek*, November 22, 1999.

78   Brammer-King: King, *None But a Blockhead*, 252–53.

78   L'Engle: *Writer's Digest*, August 1988.

79   Thurber-Peters-Mosher: Thurber, *The Years with Ross*, 33.

79   Beattie-Moore-Carson-Sobel: Yagoda, *About Town*, 387; *Publishers Weekly*, August 24, 1997; Linda Lear, *Rachel Carson: Witness for Nature* (New York: Henry Holt, 1997), 316–17; *Ruminator Review*, Spring 2002.

79–80   *New Yorker: Guardian*, October 20, 2001.

80   Frank: Bernard, *Rotten Rejections*, 37.

80   Bowles: *New Yorker*, January 15, 2001.

80   Knowles: Bernard, *Rotten Rejections*, 59.

80   Grey: Carol Gay, *Zane Grey: Story Teller* (Columbus: State Library of Ohio, 1979), 9; Ronald Weber, *Hired Pens* (Athens, Ohio: Ohio University Press, 1997), 87.

80   O'Connor: Plimpton, *Writers at Work*, 1st ser., 182.

81   Orwell: George Woodcock, *The Crystal Spirit: A Study of George Orwell* (Boston: Little, Brown, 1966), 14–15; Sonia Orwell and Ian Angus, eds., *As I Please, 1943–1945: The Collected Essays, Journalism and Letters of George Orwell*, vol. 3 (New York: Harcourt, Brace & World, 1968), 186–87; Sonia Orwell and Ian Angus, eds., *In Front of Your Nose, 1945–50: The Collected Essays, Journalism and Letters of George Orwell*, vol. 4 (New York: Harcourt, Brace & World, 1968), 109–11; Cass Canfield, *Up and Down and Around: A Publisher Recollects the Time of His Life* (New York: Harper's Magazine Press, 1971), 193; Jeffrey Meyers, *George Orwell: The Critical Heritage* (London: Routledge & Kegan Paul, 1975), 1, 19–21; Christopher Small, *The Road to Miniluv: George Orwell, the State, and God* (Pittsburgh: University of Pittsburgh Press, 1975), 101–2; Bernard Crick, *George Orwell* (Boston: Atlantic Monthly Press, 1980), 337; T. R. Fyvel, *George Orwell: A Personal Memoir* (New York: Macmillan, 1982), 129–33, 143; Michael Shelden, *Orwell: The Authorized Biography* (New York: HarperCollins, 1991), 365–69, 388; Jeffrey Meyers, *Orwell: Wintry Conscience of a Generation* (New York: Norton, 2000), 245–48, 250–52.

81   Warburg: Crick, *George Orwell*, 337.

6. *The Publishing Tribe*

83   Wolfe: Jon Winokur, ed., *Advice to Writers: A Compendium of Quotes, Anecdotes, and Writerly Wisdom from a Dazzling Array of Literary Lights* (New York: Vintage, 1999), 117.

83   Conroy: *Publishers Weekly*, September 5, 1986.

84–85 Massello: Massello, *Writer Tells All*, 188.

85   Hillerman: Tony Hillerman, *Seldom Disappointed: A Memoir* (New York: HarperCollins, 2001), 270–71; Steinberg, *Writing for Your Life*, 267; *Los Angeles Times*, January 2, 1981.

86   said one editor: *New York Times*, August 4, 2002.

87   suggested one agent: Herman, *Writer's Guide to Book Editors, Publishers, and Literary Agents 2001–2002*, 607.

87   Shaw: Plimpton, *The Writer's Chapbook*, 28; Charlton and Mark, *The Writer's Home Companion*, 102.

90   *crash, blurb, trade books*: Herman, *Writer's Guide to Book Editors, Publishers, and Literary Agents 2001–2002*, 892; Charlton and Mark, *The Writer's Home Companion*, 57, 11; *New Yorker*, October 4, 1999.

92   Beattie: Busch, *Letters to a Fiction Writer*, 57.

92   Richard Paul Evans: Jerrold R. Jenkins with Mardi Link, *Inside the Best Sellers* (Traverse City, Mich.: Rhodes & Easton, 1997), 12.

93   Zafris: *Publishers Weekly*, July 8, 2002; *Dayton Daily News*, September 8, 2002.

94   King: King, *Secret Windows*, 52.

94   Callenbach: *New York Times*, October 2, 1977; *Bookviews*, January 1978.

94   Collier: Oscar Collier with Frances Spatz Leighton, *How to Write and Sell Your First Nonfiction Book* (New York: St. Martin's, 1990), 112.

95   Berendt: *Vancouver Sun*, July 27, 1996; Lerner, *The Forest for the Trees*, 18.

95   Evans: *Publishers Weekly*, April 25, 1986.

96   Perkins: Wheelock, *Editor to Author*, 238.

96   Canfield: Canfield, *Up and Down and Around*, 204, 207.

97   Korda: Michael Korda, *Another Life* (New York: Random House, 1999), 291–92.

97   Myhre: *Los Angeles Times*, October 27, 1993.

7. Betting on Books

99   O'Shea Wade: Gerald Gross, ed., *Editors on Editing* (New York: Grove, 1993), 75.

99   Canfield: Canfield, *Up and Down and Around*, 203.

99   Rowling: *Time*, April 12, 1999; *New York Times*, October 18, 1999; *Book*, May–June 2000.

100   Oliphant: *Publishers Weekly*, October 30, 1981.

100   Jakes: *Dayton Daily News*, June 20, 1997.

101   Krantz: Cerf and Navasky, *The Experts Speak*, 180.

101   Knopf: Vanderbilt, *The Making of a Bestseller*, 120.

104–5   Geisel: Judith and Neil Morgan, *Dr. Seuss & Mr. Geisel* (New York: DaCapo Press, 1996), 82.

105   Silverstein: Cerf and Navasky, *The Experts Speak*, 178.

105   Clark: Clark, *Kitchen Privileges*, 195.

105   Stone: Charlton and Mark, *Writer's Home Companion*, 26; John White, *Rejection* (Reading, Mass.: Addison-Wesley, 1982), 2.

106   Wouk: John Tebbel, *Between Covers: The Rise and Transformation of Book Publishing in America* (New York: Oxford University Press, 1987), 357.

106   Shirer: Andre Bernard, *Now All We Need Is a Title: Famous Book Titles and How They Got That Way* (New York: Norton, 1995), 101–2.

106   Bach: *New York Times Book Review*, July 21, 1985; Cerf and Navasky, *The Experts Speak*, 180.

107   *All the President's Men*: David Obst, *Too Good to Be True: Changing America in the '60s and '70s* (New York: Wiley, 1998), 230–32.

107   *Gone with the Wind*: *New York Times*, June 10, 1984; Cerf and Navasky, *The Experts Speak*, 177.

107   King: Bernard, *Rotten Rejections*, 25.

108   Nabokov: Ibid., 70–71; *New York Times*, May 6, 1984.

108   Grisham: Oscar Collier with Frances Spatz Leighton, *How to Write and Sell Your First Novel* (Cincinnati: Writer's Digest Books, 1997), 152.

108   Rand: Barbara Branden, *The Passion of Ayn Rand* (Garden City, N.Y.: Doubleday, 1986), 169, 284.

108   Buck: Norman Cousins, *Writing for Love or Money* (New York: Longmans, Green, 1949), 73; *Dayton Daily News*, April 30, 1998.

108   White: *New York Times*, May 6, 1984; Cerf and Navasky, *The Experts Speak*, 178.

108   Auel: Bernard, *Rotten Rejections*, 14.

108   Peter: *Rotten Rejections*, 32.

108–9   Kennedy: *Publishers Weekly*, December 9, 1983; *New York Times*, September 6, 1984; William A. Gordon, ed., *The Quotable Writer: Words of Wisdom from Mark Twain, Aristotle, Oscar Wilde, Robert Frost, Erica Jong, and More* (New York: McGraw-Hill, 2000), 110.

109   Wiesel: *Publishers Weekly*, August 25, 1997.

109   Malamud: Bernard, *Rotten Rejections*, 64.

109   Forsyth: David Frost and Michael Deakin, *David Frost's Book of the World's Worst Decisions* (New York: Crown, 1983), 34–35.

109–10 Gide: William C. Carter, *Marcel Proust: A Life* (New Haven: Yale University Press, 2000), 526, 563–64; White, *Rejection*, 20; Bernard, *Rotten Rejections*, 21.

110–11 Grann: *New York Times Magazine*, April 7, 1985.

111   Wyatt: *Publishers Weekly*, September 20, 1993.

111   *The Christmas Box*: *Publishers Weekly*, May 27, 1995.

111   Orwell: Fyvel, *George Orwell*, 143; Shelden, *Orwell*, 388.

112   sales representative: Eva S. Moskowitz, *In Therapy We Trust* (Baltimore: Johns Hopkins University Press, 2001), 245.

113   Perkins: Wheelock, *Editor to Author*, 247.

113–14 Sindell: remarks by Gerald Sindell (based on his book *The Book Doctor—The Secrets of Connecting a Book to the Marketplace*), panel discussion on "Book Doctors and Bestsellers," Women's National Book Association, January 18, 2001.

8. *Encouragers*

117   Gardner: Gardner, *On Becoming a Novelist*, 109.

117   Beattie: Busch, *Letters to a Fiction Writer*, 57.

117–18 Welty-Russell: Kreyling, *Author and Agent*, 9, 23, 41, 50; Ann Waldron, *Eudora: A Writer's Life* (New York: Doubleday, 1998), 110.

118   Parini: *Some Necessary Angels*, 40.

118   McMillan-Gonshak: *New York Times*, January 28, 2001.

118   Harris: *Publishers Weekly*, July 30, 2001.

118   Grisham: Weaver, *John Grisham*, 59.

120   Clark: Clark, *Kitchen Privileges*, 9–10.

121   King: King, *Secret Windows*, 36; Underwood and Miller, *Bare Bones*, 85.

121   Orwell: Shelden, *Orwell*, 152–53.

121   Beckett: James Knowlson, *Damned to Fame: The Life of Samuel Beckett* (New York: Simon & Schuster, 1997), 340.

121 Munro: Tausky, "Alice Munro: Biocritical Essay."

121–22 McCarthy-Wilson: Plimpton, *The Writer's Chapbook*, 22.

122–23 Cannell: *Newsweek*, November 22, 1999.

123 Walker-Rukeyser: *New York Times*, October 23, 2000.

123 Turow: *Time*, June 11, 1990.

123 Gloss: *Publishers Weekly*, July 10, 2000.

123–24 Patchett: *Publishers Weekly*, October 13, 1997; Blythe, *Why I Write*, 63–68.

124 Parini: Parini, *Some Necessary Angels*, 11–13.

125 LeRoy-Gaitskill: www.jtleroy.com.

125 Fitzgerald-Bruccoli: Bruccoli and Baughman: *F. Scott Fitzgerald on Authorship*, 20, 94.

125–26 Harris-Angelou: *People*, May 15, 1995.

126 Beattie-Barthelme-Tyler: Yagoda, *About Town*, 387.

126 Lipman: *New York Times*, August 12, 2002.

126 hooks-Bambara: hooks, *remembered rapture*, 235–36.

126 Ozick: *New York Times Book Review*, February 6, 1983.

126 Roth: Plimpton, *Writers at Work*, 7th ser., 269.

126 Godwin-Irving: *New York Times Book Review*, February 6, 1983.

126 Bellow: Joyce Carol Oates, ed., *First Person Singular: Writers on Their Craft* (Princeton, N.J.: Ontario Review Press, 1983), 21.

127 Melville-Hawthorne: David Laskin, *A Common Life: Four Generations of American Literary Friendship and Influence* (New York: Simon & Schuster, 1994), 25–94.

127 Melville to Hawthorne: Ibid., 70.

127 Laskin: Ibid., 18.

127 Eliot-Pound: Gertrude Patterson, *T. S. Eliot: Poems in the Making* (New York: Manchester University Press/Barnes & Noble, 1971), 141; George Bornstein, ed., *Ezra Pound among the Poets* (Chicago: University of Chicago Press, 1985), 170–71, 192.

127 Hemingway-Fitzgerald: Bruccoli and Baughman, *F. Scott Fitzgerald on Authorship*, 20, 94; Berg, *Max Perkins*, 139.

128 Gordon: Sternburg, *The Writer on Her Work*, vol. 1, 30–31.

128 McMillan-Reed: *Newsweek*, April 29, 1996.

129 Clark: Clark, *Kitchen Privileges*, 107.

129 Tan: Tan, *The Joy Luck Club* (New York: Putnam's, 1989), unnumbered acknowledgments page.

131 Lukeman: "One Woman's Writing Retreat," interview with C. T. Atherton (Catherine Tudor), 2002, www.prairieden.com.

131 Sparks: *Stuart News*, December 14, 1997; *Book Publishing Report*, February 11, 2002.

131   Harrison: *Entertainment Weekly*, August 24, 1990.
131   Krichevsky: AuthorsOnTheWeb.com.
132   Steel: Vickie L. Bane and Lorenzo Benet, *The Lives of Danielle Steel* (New York: St. Martin's, 1994; reprint, 1995), 38.
132   Moore: *Publishers Weekly*, November 6, 1995.
132   Michener: James Michener, *The World Is My Home: A Memoir* (New York: Random House, 1992), 283–89.
132   Quinn: *Booknook*, WYSO-FM (Yellow Springs, Ohio), November 13, 1997; *Publishers Weekly*, June 12, 2000, September 3, 2001.
133   Perkins-Wolfe: Lerner, *The Forest for the Trees*, 200.
133   Didion-Robbins: Joan Didion, *After Henry* (New York: Simon & Schuster, 1992), 20.
134   Gallant: Gallant, *Selected Short Stories*, xix.
134   King-Thompson: Tim Underwood and Chuck Miller, *Kingdom of Fear: The World of Stephen King* (New York: New American Library, 1986), 31; King, *Secret Windows*, 36, 42–43.
134   Butler: *Publishers Weekly*, January 1, 1982.
134   Rice: Ibid., September 20, 1993.
135   Brown: Bonetti et al., *Conversations with American Novelists*, 250–51.
136   Korda: Korda, *Another Life*, 73–74.
136–37 Disney: *New Yorker*, October 6, 1997.
138   Cheever: Plimpton, *The Writer's Chapbook*, 91–92.
138   King: Underwood and Miller, *Bare Bones*, 59.
138   hooks: hooks, *remembered rapture*, 150–52.
139   Proust: Marcel Proust, *On Reading*, ed. and trans. Jean Autret and William Burford (New York: Macmillan, 1971), 55; Alain de Botton, *How Proust Can Change Your Life* (London: Picador, 1997), 138–39.

9. Keeping Hope Alive

140   Ellison: Beahm, *The Stephen King Companion*, 152.
140   Hospital: Busch, *Letters to a Fiction Writer*, 184.
140–41 Busch-Lowry: Busch, *A Dangerous Profession*, 74–75.
141   Targ: Deirdre Bair, *Samuel Beckett: A Biography* (New York: Harcourt Brace Jovanovich, 1978), 270; *New York Times*, December 11, 1981.
142   Godwin: *New York Times Book Review*, July 21, 1985.
142   Thackeray: Keith Gessen discussing David Markson's novel *Reader's Block*, "Writing for No Body," www.kraus99.com.

142 Kipling: Frost and Deakin, *David Frost's Book of the World's Worst Decisions*, ix.

142 Lebowitz: *Fresh Air* (National Public Radio), January 31, 1996.

142–43 Woolf: Woolf, *A Writer's Diary*, 21, 14.

143–44 Ryan: Terry Ryan, *The Prizewinner of Defiance, Ohio* (New York: Simon & Schuster, 2001).

144 Torrey: Joanna Torrey, *Hungry* (New York: Crown, 1998).

144 de Botton: de Botton, *How Proust Can Change Your Life*.

144 Eddy: Paul Eddy, *Flint* (New York: Putnam, 2001).

144 Shields: *Unless*.

144 Proust: Rosellen Brown, *Before and After* (Farrar Straus & Giroux, 1992), 94; de Botton, *How Proust Can Change Your Life*, 117, 131.

146 Flagg-Ferrigno-Allende: *Authors Guild Bulletin*, Winter 1995; *Orange County Register*, March 11, 1990; *USA Today*, July 1, 1991.

146 Tan: *Boston Globe*, June 21, 1991; Judith Appelbaum, *How to Get Happily Published* (New York: HarperPerennial, 1998), 54, Katherine Usher Henderson, ed., *Inter/View:Talks with America's Writing Women* (Lexington, Ky.: University of Kentucky Press, 1990), 19.

146 Auel: *My Generation*, September–October 2002.

146 Harris: *Publishers Weekly*, December 18, 2000.

148 Flaubert: *The Selected Letters of Gustave Flaubert*, 177–78.

150 Krichevsky: AuthorsOnTheWeb.com.

151 Sherwood: *Newsweek*, June 7, 1993.

151 Kipling: Plimpton, *Writers at Work*, 1st ser., 17.

151 Steinbeck: Plimpton, *The Writer's Chapbook*, 120.

152 Kunitz: Plimpton, *The Writer's Chapbook*, 79.

152 Wallace: Blythe, *Why I Write*, 140–41.

152 Ovid: W. Francis H. King, *Classical and Foreign Quotations: A Polyglot Dictionary of Historical and Literary Quotations, Proverbs and Popular Sayings* (New York: Frederick Ungar, 1958), 285.

152–53 Lebowitz: *Harper's*, November 1993, 34.

153 Hemingway: Plimpton, *Writers at Work*, 2nd ser., 219.

153 Burgess: *All Things Considered* (National Public Radio), November 25, 1993; *U.S. News & World Report*, December 6, 1993.

153 Shaw-Wambaugh: *Horizon*, December 1980; *Writer's Digest*, December 1973.

153 Waugh-Mailer-Thurber-Wodehouse: George Plimpton, ed., *Writers at Work*, 3rd ser. (New York: Viking, 1967), 10, 257; Winokur, *Writers on Writing*, 102; Plimpton, *Writers at Work*, 5th ser., 6.

153   Caldwell: Plimpton, *The Writer's Chapbook*, 51.

153–54 Haruf: *New York Times*, December 1, 1999.

154   Wolfe: *People*, September 20, 1982.

154   Wilde: Robert Harborough Sherard, *Oscar Wilde: The Story of an Unhappy Friendship* (London: Hermes Press, 1902; New York: Haskell, 1970), 26.

154   Munro-Bainbridge: *New York Times*, November 30, 1998; *Publishers Weekly*, November 9, 1998.

154   Grimes: *Washington Post*, November 30, 1999.

154   Redfield: *People*, April 25, 1994.

154   Parini: Parini, *Some Necessary Angels*, 41.

154   Bellow: Atlas, *Bellow*, 462.

155   Atwood: Atwood, *Negotiating with the Dead*, xx–xxii.

156   Gaitskill: Blythe, *Why I Write*, 158.

156   Roth: Plimpton, *Writers at Work*, 7th ser., 273.

156   Lawrence: *Psychology Today*, December 1968; Winokur, *Writers on Writing*, 129.

156   Gass: Plimpton, *Writers at Work*, 5th ser., 273.

156   Stein-Faulkner-Salter: Salter in Blythe, *Why I Write*, 39.

156–57 Grisham-Grafton: *Newsweek*, May 8, 1995; Shaughnessy, *Walking on Alligators*, 172; *Publishers Weekly*, May 5, 1989.

157   Hawkes: Murray, *Shoptalk*, 5.

157   Gardner: Gardner, *On Becoming a Novelist*, 137.

157   Diamant: *Newsweek*, February 5, 2001; *Publishers Weekly*, March 26, 2001.

158   Grisham: Weaver, *John Grisham*, 36; *Dayton Daily News*, February 11, 1999.

159–60 McMillan: *People*, December 28, 1997–January 4, 1993; *Newsweek*, April 29, 1996; Lerner, *The Forest for the Trees*, 268–69.

10. The Best of Times

161   Epstein: *Authors Guild Bulletin*, Fall 2000.

161   Atlas: *Los Angeles Times*, February 25, 2001.

161   the study: Jenkins Group, Inc., press release, PRNewswire, September 23, 2002.

161–62 Gibson: *Los Angeles Times*, February 25, 2001.

162   Gallup Poll: *Newsweek*, July 17, 2000.

162   Despite all the dire predictions: *Time*, April 21, 1997; *New Yorker*, October 6, 1997; *New York Times*, July 12, 1999; *Atlantic Monthly*,

July–August 2001; *Time*, October 21, 2002; *Publishers Weekly*, January 6, 2003, March 10, 2003.

165   Bush: *Publishers Weekly*, April 29, 2002.

165   Wiesel-Clancy-Coonts: *Publishers Weekly*, August 25, 1997; *New York Times*, April 13, 1988.

165   Beckett-Grove: Knowlson, *Damned to Fame*, 269.

165   Sorrentino-Grove: *Publishers Weekly*, May 27, 2002.

165   The consolidation of publishers: *New Yorker*, October 6, 1997; *Publishers Weekly*, December 22, 1997; *Atlantic Monthy*, July–August 2001; *Christian Science Monitor*, April 16, 2002; *Publishers Weekly*, October 21, 2002.

166   Herman: Herman, *Writer's Guide to Book Editors, Publishers, and Literary Agents 2001–2002*, 738–39.

167   Pearlman: *Publishers Weekly*, September 11, 2000.

168   Branon: *People*, April 18, 1994.

170   Thoreau: Charlton and Mark, *The Writer's Home Companion*, 15–16.

170   Potter: White, *Rejection*, 1; Frost and Deakin, *David Frost's Book of the World's Worst Decisions*, 32.

170–71   *Robert's-Bartlett's-Joy*: Collier with Leighton, *How to Write and Sell Your First Nonfiction Book*, 228; White, *Rejection*, 11.

171   Edward FitzGerald: Bernard, *Rotten Rejections*, 70.

171   Nin: Arthur T. Vanderbilt, *The Making of a Bestseller* (Jefferson, N.C.: McFarland, 1999), 106.

171   Crane: Charlton and Mark, *The Writer's Home Companion*, 22.

171   Hoeye: *Seattle Post-Intelligencer*, March 5, 2002.

171   Evans: Jenkins with Link, *Inside the Bestsellers*, 31.

171   Callenbach: *New York Times*, October 2, 1977; *Bookviews*, January 1978.

172   E. Lynn Harris: *People*, May 15, 1995; *Publishers Weekly*, July 23, 2001, July 30, 2001.

172–73   Warner executive: *Publishers Weekly*, May 22, 1995.

173   Zagat: *New York Times*, November 11, 1998.

176   Zane: *Publishers Weekly*, July 15, 2002.

177–79   Epstein: Jason Epstein, *Book Business* (New York: Norton, 2001), 181, 109; *Publishers Weekly*, January 1, 2001.

11. The Hopeful Writer

180   White: Plimpton, *Writers at Work*, 8th ser., 8, 23.

181   Targ: Literature Resource Center, galenet.galegroup.com.

181   Melville: *Herman Melville: Damned in Paradise*, The Film Company, 1986; William Safire and Leonard Safir, *Good Advice on Writing* (New York: Fireside/Simon & Schuster, 1993), 14.

182–83 Gardner: Gardner, *On Becoming a Novelist*, 70.

183   Huxley: Aldous Huxley, *Point Counter Point* (Garden City, N.Y.: Doubleday Doran, 1928; Modern Library, 1938), 194.

183   Flaubert: *The Selected Letters of Gustave Flaubert*, 143, 166.

184   someone once observed: Lesley Conger, *Writer*, June 1977.

184   Porter: Isabel Bayley, ed., *Letters of Katherine Anne Porter* (New York: Atlantic Monthly Press, 1990), 562.

184   Spencer: Elizabeth Spencer, *Landscapes of the Heart: A Memoir* (New York: Random House, 1998), 195.

184   Smith: Blythe, *Why I Write*, 134–35.

184–85 Kafka: Leon Edel, *Stuff of Sleep and Dreams: Experiments in Literary Psychology*. (New York: Harper & Row, 1982), 127.

185   Gardner: Gardner, *On Becoming a Novelist*, 145.

185–86 Dickinson: Thomas H. Johnson, ed., *The Complete Poems of Emily Dickinson* (Boston: Little, Brown, 1899, 1960), poems 288, 709, pp. 133, 348–49; Alfred Habegger, *My Wars Are Laid Away in Books: The Life of Emily Dickinson* (New York: Random House, 2001), 629.

186–87 Flaubert: Steegmuller, *The Selected Letters of Gustave Flaubert*, 43, 201.

188   Amis: Plimpton, *Writers at Work*, 5th ser., 197.

188   Mitchell: Al Silverman, ed., *The Book-of-the-Month: Sixty Years of Books in American Life* (Boston: Little, Brown, 1986), 47.

188   Conroy: Associated Press, November 14, 1986.

188   Kazin: Jacob M. Braude, *Braude's Source Book for Speakers and Writers* (Englewood Cliffs, N.J.: Prentice Hall, 1968), 24.

188   Cheever: *The Journals of John Cheever*, ix.

188   Oe: *Dayton Daily News*, October 14, 1994.

188   Lawrence: Jeffrey Meyers, *Hemingway: A Biography* (New York: Harper & Row, 1985), 136.

188   McMillan: Blythe, *Why I Write*, 70–72.

188   a group of patients: *Journal of the American Medical Association*, April 14, 1999, 1304–9.

189   Greene: Murray, *Shoptalk*, 5.

189   King: King, *Secret Windows*, 14, 245, 386; Beahm, *The Stephen King Companion*, 36; King, *On Writing*, 249.

Further Reading

A number of books on writing have been written in a spirit like this one, and I recommend them for further reading.

Stephen King's *On Writing: A Memoir of the Craft* (New York: Scribner, 2000) is a lively, compassionate, but hardheaded account of the writer's life. Margaret Atwood's *Negotiating with the Dead: A Writer on Writing* (Cambridge: Cambridge University Press, 2002) includes unique insights on the writer's world, as does John Gardner's classic *On Becoming a Novelist* (New York: Norton, 1983, 1999), which includes a good foreword by Raymond Carver. Anne Lamott's *Bird by Bird: Some Instructions on Writing and Life* (New York: Pantheon, 1994) is a quirky, insightful, and often hilarious depiction of what it means to be a writer. Betsy Lerner's *The Forest for the Trees: An Editor's Advice to Writers* (New York: Riverhead, 2000) has a similar flavor and the added benefit of being written from the perspective of a former editor. Among the many books of affirmations and meditations for writers, Susan Shaughnessy's *Walking on Alligators: A Book of Meditations for Writers* (San Francisco: HarperSanFrancisco, 1993) is best-of-show.

Frederick Busch's *A Dangerous Profession: A Book about the Writing Life* (New York: St. Martin's, 1998; Broadway, 1999) and the compilation he edited called *Letters to a Fiction Writer* (New York: Norton, 1999) incorporate humane insights on the writer's world and how that world can be navigated. In the latter, essays by George Garrett, Janette Turner Hospital, and Charles Baxter stand out, as does Busch's introduction. Will Blythe's *Why I Write: Thoughts on the Craft of Fiction* (Boston: Little, Brown, 1998) is another excellent anthology of writing about writing, especially the essays by Ann Patchett, Lee Smith, and David Foster Wallace.

Some other essays on this subject that I found particularly thoughtful are one by Theodore Solotaroff ("Writing in the Cold," in Solotaroff's *A Few Good Voices in My Head: Occasional Pieces on Writing, Editing, and Reading My Contemporaries* [New York: Harper & Row, 1987]) and two by Gail Godwin ("A Writing Woman," *Atlantic Monthly*, October 1979, reprinted as "Becoming a Writer" in Janet Sternburg, ed., *The Writer on Her Work* [New York: Norton, 1980] and "Rituals and Readiness: Getting Ready to Write," in National Book Award authors, *The Writing Life: A Collection of Essays and Interviews* [New York: Random House, 1995]). Just about anything Godwin writes on writing is worth reading. So are Cynthia Ozick's comments in interviews, such as the one she did with *Paris Review* (in George Plimpton, ed., *Writers at Work*, 8th ser. [New York: Viking, 1988]).

The *Paris Review* interviews with writers are uniformly excellent, a great resource for writers who are curious about other writers. They are compiled in anthologies called *Writers at Work*. A sampling of their contents, organized by topic ("Work Habits," "Writer's Block," "Inspiration," "Sex," etc.), can be found in George Plimpton, ed., *The Writer's Chapbook: A Compendium of Fact, Opinion, Wit, and Advice from the 20th Century's Preeminent Writers* (New York: Viking, 1989).

As its subtitle suggests, *The Writer's Home Companion: Anecdotes, Comforts, Recollections and Other Amusements for Every Writer, Editor and Reader* by James Charlton and Lisbeth Mark (New York: Franklin Watts, 1987) is a pleasing compilation of miscellany about writers and their lives. So is Robert Hendrickson's *The Literary Life and Other Curiosities: A Compendium of Facts and Fictions about Writers and Writing, Books and Blurbs, Arts and Letters* (New York: Viking, 1981).

As suggested in the text, published diaries, journals, and letters of writers can be wonderfully reassuring to readers who wonder if noted authors ever got discouraged too. For this book, *The Letters of John Cheever* (Benjamin Cheever, ed.; New York: Simon & Schuster, 1988) and *The Journals of John Cheever* (New York: Knopf, 1991) were particularly helpful, as were *The Selected Letters of Gustave Flaubert* (Francis Steegmuller, ed.; New York: Farrar Straus & Giroux, 1953; reprinted by Books for Libraries Press, 1971), Virginia Woolf's *A Writer's Diary* (Leonard Woolf, ed.; New York: Harcourt Brace Jovanovich, 1953), and *F. Scott Fitzgerald on Authorship* (Matthew J. Bruccoli and Judith S. Baugham, eds., Columbia, S.C.: University of South Carolina Press, 1996). Carol Edgarian and Tom Jenks, *The Writer's Life: Intimate Thoughts on Work, Love, Inspiration, and Fame from the Diaries of the World's Great Writers* (New York: Vintage, 1997) is a sampling of excerpts from writers' journals, organized topically under headings such as "Inspiration," "Success and Failure," and "Self-Doubt."

Judy Mandell's *Book Editors Talk to Writers* (New York: Wiley, 1995) and John F. Baker's *Literary Agents: A Writer's Introduction* (New York: Macmillan, 1999) are useful resources for getting the perspective of agents and editors. Michael Korda's memoir, *Another Life* (New York: Random House, 1999), is an illuminating look at the world of editors and publishing, and also a good read. The literary agent Noah Lukeman provides helpful advice in *The First Five Pages: A Writer's Guide to Staying out of the Rejection Pile* (New York: Fireside/Simon & Schuster, 2000).

Rejection is a subject too seldom considered in writing about writers. A rare exception is an excellent article on this topic in the *New York Times Book Review* of July 21, 1985, by Barbara Bauer and Robert F. Moss, who compiled thoughts on this subject from a remarkable roster of well-known writers. As noted in the text, reading *Rotten Rejections: A Literary Companion*, a compilation of rejection letter excerpts edited by Andre Bernard (Wainscott, N.Y.: Pushcart Press, 1990), is a comfort. *Rotten Rejections* draws in part on accounts of rejected famous writers in John White's *Rejection* (Reading, Mass.: Addison-Wesley, 1982). Sophy Burnham's *For Writers Only* (New York: Ballantine, 1996) has a section on "Rejection," as well as ones on "Aloneness," "Jealousy," and "Alcohol, Depression, Drugs, Suicide."

Judith Appelbaum's *How to Get Happily Published* (New York: HarperCollins, 1998) remains the gold standard for books of its kind. John Boswell's *The Insider's Guide to Getting Published* (originally titled *The Awful Truth about Publishing* [New York: Doubleday, 1997]) is also quite helpful. Jeff Herman's *Writer's Guide to Book Editors, Publishers, and Literary Agents* (Roseville, Calif.: Prima Publishing, updated annually) is a gold mine of useful information and includes an excellent glossary of pub-speak.

Arthur T. Vanderbilt's *The Making of a Bestseller* (Jefferson, N.C.: McFarland, 1999) incorporates many accounts of noted writers' travails. *Inside the Bestsellers*, by Jerrold R. Jenkins with Mardi Link (Traverse City, Mich.: Rhodes & Easton, 1997), gathers accounts of writers such as Richard Paul Evans and Betty Eadie whose successful books were originally self-published or published by very small presses.

As indicated in the text, *Book Business* by Jason Epstein (New York: Norton, 2001) foresees a brave new publishing world with vastly expanded opportunities for writers to reach readers.

Index

About the Author

RALPH KEYES is the author of ten books and numerous articles that have appeared in publications such as *Newsweek, Harper's, GQ, Glamour, Sports Illustrated,* and *Writer's Digest.* A writing teacher for more than thirty years, Keyes is a trustee of the Antioch Writers' Workshop.